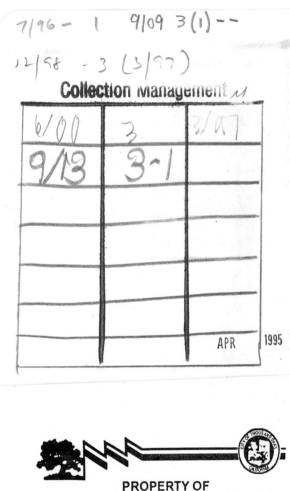

7/96 - 1   9/09 3(1)--

12/98 - 3 (3/97)

Collection Management

6/00	3	3/97
9/13	3-1	

APR 1995

Lt. Charles Wilkes
and the Great U.S. Exploring Expedition

General Editor

William H. Goetzmann
Jack S. Blanton, Sr., Chair in History
    University of Texas at Austin

Consulting Editor

Tom D. Crouch
Chairman, Department of Aeronautics
    National Air and Space Museum
    Smithsonian Institution

WORLD EXPLORERS

Lt. Charles Wilkes
and the Great U.S. Exploring Expedition

Cheri Wolfe

Introductory Essay by Michael Collins

CHELSEA HOUSE PUBLISHERS

New York • Philadelphia

On the cover Map of Pacific islands; portrait of Lt.
Charles Wilkes

Chelsea House Publishers
Editor-in-Chief Remmel Nunn
Managing Editor Karyn Gullen Browne
Copy Chief Juliann Barbato
Picture Editor Adrian G. Allen
Art Director Maria Epes
Deputy Copy Chief Mark Rifkin
Assistant Art Director Noreen Romano
Series Design Loraine Machlin
Manufacturing Manager Gerald Levine
Systems Manager Lindsey Ottman
Production Manager Joseph Romano
Production Coordinator Marie Claire Cebrián

World Explorers
Senior Editor Sean Dolan

Staff for LT. CHARLES WILKES AND THE GREAT U.S. EXPLORING EXPEDITION
Associate Editor Terrance Dolan
Copy Editor Benson D. Simmonds
Editorial Assistant Martin Mooney
Picture Researcher Alan Gottlieb
Senior Designer Basia Niemczyc

First Printing

1 3 5 7 9 8 6 4 2

Library of Congress Cataloging-in-Publication Data

Wolfe, Cheri
   Lt. Charles Wilkes and the great U.S. Exploring Expedition/
Cheri Wolfe.
      p. cm.—(World explorers)
   Includes bibliographical references and index.
   Summary: Describes the journey of Charles Wilkes as he led a
group of American seamen through the South Pacific and became
the first to cite Antarctica as a separate continent.
   ISBN 0-7910-1320-0
         0-7910-1545-9
   1. United States Exploring Expedition (1838–42)—Juvenile
literature.   2. Voyages around the world—Juvenile literature.
3. Wilkes, Charles, 1798–1877—Juvenile literature. [1. United
States Exploring Expedition (1838–42)   2. Wilkes, Charles,
1798–1877.   3. Explorers.] I. Title.   II. Title: Lieutenant
Charles Wilkes and the great U.S. Exploring Expedition.
III. Series
                                                    91-8490
G420.U55W65 1991   CIP
910′.91648—dc20   AC

CONTENTS

WORLD EXPLORERS

THE EARLY EXPLORERS

Herodotus and the Explorers of the Classical Age
Marco Polo and the Medieval Explorers
The Viking Explorers

THE FIRST GREAT AGE OF DISCOVERY

Jacques Cartier, Samuel de Champlain, and the Explorers of Canada
Christopher Columbus and the First Voyages to the New World
From Coronado to Escalante: The Explorers of the Spanish Southwest
Hernando de Soto and the Explorers of the American South
Sir Francis Drake and the Struggle for an Ocean Empire
Vasco da Gama and the Portuguese Explorers
La Salle and the Explorers of the Mississippi
Ferdinand Magellan and the Discovery of the World Ocean
Pizarro, Orellana, and the Exploration of the Amazon
The Search for the Northwest Passage
Giovanni da Verrazano and the Explorers of the Atlantic Coast

THE SECOND GREAT AGE OF DISCOVERY

Roald Amundsen and the Quest for the South Pole
Daniel Boone and the Opening of the Ohio Country
Captain James Cook and the Explorers of the Pacific
The Explorers of Alaska
John Charles Frémont and the Great Western Reconnaissance
Alexander von Humboldt, Colossus of Exploration
Lewis and Clark and the Route to the Pacific
Alexander Mackenzie and the Explorers of Canada
Robert Peary and the Quest for the North Pole
Zebulon Pike and the Explorers of the American Southwest
John Wesley Powell and the Great Surveys of the American West
Jedediah Smith and the Mountain Men of the American West
Henry Stanley and the European Explorers of Africa
Lt. Charles Wilkes and the Great U.S. Exploring Expedition

THE THIRD GREAT AGE OF DISCOVERY

Apollo to the Moon
The Explorers of the Undersea World
The First Men in Space
The Mission to Mars and Beyond
Probing Deep Space

CHELSEA HOUSE PUBLISHERS

Into the Unknown

Michael Collins

It is difficult to define most eras in history with any precision, but not so the space age. On October 4, 1957, it burst on us with little warning when the Soviet Union launched *Sputnik*, a 184-pound cannonball that circled the globe once every 96 minutes. Less than 4 years later, the Soviets followed this first primitive satellite with the flight of Yuri Gagarin, a 27-year-old fighter pilot who became the first human to orbit the earth. The Soviet Union's success prompted President John F. Kennedy to decide that the United States should "land a man on the moon and return him safely to earth" before the end of the 1960s. We now had not only a space age but a space race.

I was born in 1930, exactly the right time to allow me to participate in Project Apollo, as the U.S. lunar program came to be known. As a young man growing up, I often found myself too young to do the things I wanted—or suddenly too old, as if someone had turned a switch at midnight. But for Apollo, 1930 was the perfect year to be born, and I was very lucky. In 1966 I enjoyed circling the earth for three days, and in 1969 I flew to the moon and laughed at the sight of the tiny earth, which I could cover with my thumbnail.

How the early explorers would have loved the view from space! With one glance Christopher Columbus could have plotted his course and reassured his crew that the world was indeed round. In 90 minutes Magellan could have looked down at every port of call in the *Victoria's* three-year circumnavigation of the globe. Given a chance to map their route from orbit, Lewis and Clark could have told President Jefferson that there was no easy Northwest Passage but that a continent of exquisite diversity awaited their scrutiny.

In a physical sense, we have already gone to most places that we can. That is not to say that there are not new adventures awaiting us deep in the sea or on the red plains of Mars, but more important than reaching new places will be understanding those we have already visited. There are vital gaps in our understanding of how our planet works as an ecosystem and how our planet fits into the infinite order of the universe. The next great age may well be the age of assimilation, in which we use microscope and telescope to evaluate what we have discovered and put that knowledge to use. The adventure of being first to reach may be replaced by the satisfaction of being first to grasp. Surely that is a form of exploration as vital to our well-being, and perhaps even survival, as the distinction of being the first to explore a specific geographical area.

The explorers whose stories are told in the books of this series did not just sail perilous seas, scale rugged mountains, traverse blistering deserts, dive to the depths of the ocean, or land on the moon. Their voyages and expeditions were journeys of mind as much as of time and distance, through which they—and all of mankind—were able to reach a greater understanding of our universe. That challenge remains, for all of us. The imperative is to see, to understand, to develop knowledge that others can use, to help nurture this planet that sustains us all. Perhaps being born in 1975 will be as lucky for a new generation of explorer as being born in 1930 was for Neil Armstrong, Buzz Aldrin, and Mike Collins.

The Reader's Journey

William H. Goetzmann

This volume is one of a series that takes us with the great explorers of the ages on bold journeys over the oceans and the continents and into outer space. As we travel along with these imaginative and courageous journeyers, we share their adventures and their knowledge. We also get a glimpse of that mysterious and inextinguishable fire that burned in the breast of men such as Magellan and Columbus—the fire that has propelled all those throughout the ages who have been driven to leave behind family and friends for a voyage into the unknown.

No one has ever satisfactorily explained the urge to explore, the drive to go to the "back of beyond." It is certain that it has been present in man almost since he began walking erect and first ventured across the African savannas. Sparks from that same fire fueled the transoceanic explorers of the Ice Age, who led their people across the vast plain that formed a land bridge between Asia and North America, and the astronauts and scientists who determined that man must reach the moon.

Besides an element of adventure, all exploration involves an element of mystery. We must not confuse exploration with discovery. Exploration is a purposeful human activity—a search for something. Discovery may be the end result of that search; it may also be an accident, as when Columbus found a whole new world while search-ing for the Indies. Often, the explorer may not even realize the full significance of what he has discovered, as was the case with Columbus. Exploration, on the other hand, is the product of a cultural or individual curiosity; it is a unique process that has enabled mankind to know and understand the world's oceans, continents, and polar re-gions. It is at the heart of scientific thinking. One of its most significant aspects is that it teaches people to ask the right questions; by doing so, it forces us to reevaluate what we think we know and understand. Thus knowledge pro-gresses, and we are driven constantly to a new awareness and appreciation of the universe in all its infinite variety.

The motivation for exploration is not always pure. In his fascination with the new, man often forgets that others have been there before him. For example, the popular notion of the discovery of America overlooks the complex Indian civilizations that had existed there for thousands of years before the arrival of Europeans. Man's desire for conquest, riches, and fame is often linked inextricably with his quest for the unknown, but a story that touches so closely on the human essence must of necessity treat war as well as peace, avarice with generosity, both pride and humility, frailty and greatness. The story of exploration is above all a story of humanity and of man's understanding of his place in the universe.

The WORLD EXPLORERS series has been divided into four sections. The first treats the explorers of the ancient world, the Viking explorers of the 9th through the 11th centuries, and Marco Polo and the medieval explorers. The rest of the series is divided into three great ages of exploration. The first is the era of Columbus and Magellan: the period spanning the 15th and 16th centuries, which saw the dis-covery and exploration of the New World and the world ocean. The second might be called the age of science and imperialism, the era made possible by the scientific ad-vances of the 17th century, which witnessed the discovery of the world's last two undiscovered continents, Australia and Antarctica, the mapping of all the continents and oceans, and the establishment of colonies all over the world. The third great age refers to the most ambitious quests of the 20th century—the probing of space and of the ocean's depths.

As we reach out into the darkness of outer space and other galaxies, we come to better understand how our ancestors confronted *oecumene*, or the vast earthly unknown. We learn once again the meaning of an unknown 18th-century sea captain's advice to navigators:

> And if by chance you make a landfall on the shores of another sea in a far country inhabited by savages and barbarians, remember you this: the greatest danger and the surest hope lies not with fires and arrows but in the quicksilver hearts of men.

At its core, exploration is a series of moral dramas. But it is these dramas, involving new lands, new people, and exotic ecosystems of staggering beauty, that make the explorers' stories not only moral tales but also some of the greatest adventure stories ever recorded. They represent the process of learning in its most expansive and vivid forms. We see that real life, past and present, transcends even the adventures of the starship *Enterprise*.

An Admiral Foreordained

On December 26, 1839, four tall-masted sailing ships weighed anchor from Sydney, Australia. The vessels, under the command of Lieutenant Charles Wilkes, an ambitious, meticulous, hard-driving, at times tyrannical officer, constituted the United States South Seas Exploring Expedition, the most far reaching scientific and exploratory venture yet conceived by the young republic. On this day, despite several indications that to do so was foolhardy, the fleet was bound south, to make its second attempt to reach Antarctica and become the first to conclusively demonstrate that that icy region was indeed a continent. The Australians, who had seen many confident captains depart their shores for the Antarctic, warned the Americans that their ships were too flimsy to challenge the southern pack ice, an admonition confirmed by the Exploring Expedition's own carpenters, who informed Wilkes that the timbers on at least two of the vessels—the sloop-of-war *Peacock* and the schooner *Flying Fish*—were rotting away. The expedition lacked much of the standard equipment for polar missions, including adequate winter clothing for its crew, and its ships could carry only enough coal to fuel its primitive heaters for seven months, which would not be nearly enough should they become trapped in the ice for the duration of a polar winter. After learning from the carpenters that the necessary repairs would take two

Lieutenant Charles Wilkes was just two weeks shy of his 40th birthday when he was offered command of the United States South Seas Exploring Expedition. He was determined to follow his orders for the voyage, in his own words, "to such a degree that no person shall ever be able to say I ought to have done more."

months—exactly the time left in Antarctica's brief summer—Wilkes decided to press on regardless, judging the potential rewards to be worth the considerable risk. He ordered his fleet to sail south "as far as the ice will permit."

Six days out of port, on the afternoon of New Year's Day, the fleet sailed into a gale. Gusting northerly winds slammed into the four elegant sailing vessels, and a thick fog shrouded the sea. The *Flying Fish*, at 96 tons the smallest of the ships, suffered a split topsail, broke the jaws of its gaff (a stout wooden pole used to support the rigging), and lost its jib sheet, leaving it essentially crippled and at the mercy of the raging elements. Two of its sister ships—the *Peacock* and the *Porpoise*—vanished into the thickening fog, but a member of the crew of the *Flying Fish* was able to spot the flagship *Vincennes*, under the personal command of Wilkes. As the horrified lookout watched through his spyglass, Wilkes mercilessly signaled the disabled ship to "make sail" and then sailed away. The *Vincennes*, according to George Sinclair, a member of the crew, "deliberately left us to whatever fate the gods of the Winds might have in store." "A few deep toned curses," he continued, "accompanied her."

As black storm clouds loom menacingly on the horizon, the Peacock *drifts helplessly, stern first, toward what its captain and crew feared would be a fatal collision with a towering ice barrier off the coast of Antarctica during the expedition's second polar voyage in 1840. This illustration, which first appeared in Wilkes's five-volume narrative of the voyage, is a steel engraving based upon the work of Alfred Agate, an artist who sailed with the expedition.*

A controversial figure for most of his 79 years, Charles Wilkes was born in New York City on April 3, 1798. He was the youngest of five children. The family was of English descent and claimed several ancestors of distinction. Charles's father, John Deponthieu Wilkes, immigrated to the American colonies during the revolutionary war. A successful businessman, he was able to provide a gracious standard of living for his family. Charles's mother, Mary Seton, died when he was only three years old. Among the numerous female relatives, friends, and retainers who then helped raise him was his aunt Elizabeth Seton, who in 1974 was canonized as the first American saint of the Roman Catholic church. She cared for Wilkes only a short time, however, and few who knew him in later life would have professed that they saw much of her influence in his character. Certainly, neither detractor nor admirer ever described Charles Wilkes as saintly.

Mary Reed, a Welsh woman whom Wilkes described later as his nurse and foster mother, exerted a much greater influence on him. "Mammy" Reed believed that she possessed the gift of prophecy. Some called her a witch; in his autobiography, which was not published during his lifetime, Wilkes commented on her "peculiar piercing" eyes and observed that she had a "swarthy dark gipsy complexion and ruddy strong look." She predicted great things for her charge—that he would go to sea and become an admiral, a rank that did not then exist in the U.S. Navy.

At age four, Charles was sent off to school. Over the next several years, he attended a succession of boarding schools, where he studied languages, mathematics, and drawing, and he developed into a handsome youth with brown hair, dark eyes, an aquiline nose, and a full mouth. At age 15, while attending a preparatory school for Columbia College (now Columbia University), he first made known his wish to go to sea. Despite his father's objection, his "hankering after naval life & a roving lifestyle grew stronger & stronger," according to the autobiography.

Wilkes's father, John Deponthieu Wilkes, was a successful businessman in New York City who had emigrated from England. Although he initially disapproved of his son's desire for a naval career, he eventually helped Wilkes obtain an appointment in the navy.

As those who served under him would later learn, Wilkes was not easily dissuaded once he set his mind on a course of action. With tutoring from John Garnett, the editor of the *American Nautical Almanac,* he studied charts and learned basic navigational principles, and his father relented and agreed to help his son obtain a midshipman's appointment in the navy. Impatient, Wilkes in the meantime signed on as a hand aboard the *Hibernia,* a merchant ship owned by family friends and bound for France. The senior Wilkes hoped that the voyage would end his son's love affair with the sea.

On board the *Hibernia,* Wilkes's youthful infatuation blossomed into a mature romance that was destined to last a lifetime, but he endured a rough coming-of-age. The old salts aboard the *Hibernia* were quick to disabuse him of his admittedly "high idea" of his own self-worth, and he initially found himself unprepared for shipboard life. He was often the target of the notoriously blistering and creative profanity used by seagoing men, and he complained in letters to his father that the ropes of the rigging made his hands bleed. Several members of the crew decided to christen him as a sailor by covering his rosy cheeks with tar. Although he was made miserable by such treatment, Wilkes delighted in the sea and the intricacies of handling a ship, and his abilities were such that when the captain confided that he had left New York without his navigational charts, Wilkes was able to draw him one of the English Channel. He was given increased responsibilities, and his determination to become a sailor remained unaltered. After making another voyage to France, this time aboard a merchant vessel called the *Emulation,* he received his appointment as a midshipman in the U.S. Navy.

His initial posting, which came in late January 1818, was to the *Independence,* then anchored in Boston Harbor, where he and about 50 other "mids" received 6 months of officer's training. This brief introduction was enough to convince Wilkes that "a midshipman's life on board a[n] American Man of war was a dog's life." He observed that "captains thought that they were above the law and no regulations bound them to observe a proper regard for the feelings and sensibilities." On his first voyage as a navy midshipman, aboard the *Guerriere*, which was carrying diplomats to their posts in Russia and Scandinavia, he demonstrated a ready grasp of sailing technique that impressed his captain. He also contracted malaria, but during his convalescence back home in New York City he hired tutors to advance his understanding of mathematics, engineering, and drawing. On his next voyage, to South America aboard the *Franklin*, he had his first experience at long-term command when he took charge in Valparaiso, Chile, of the *O'Cain*, a merchant ship whose captain had died, and guided it safely around treacherous Cape Horn and back to its home port of Boston. Earlier on that same voyage, Wilkes had briefly commanded a newly constructed vessel, the *Waterwitch*, for the duration of a brief voyage in Chilean coastal waters.

Members of the peacetime navy often went long periods at a time on leave awaiting their next posting, and Wilkes spent the next several years in New York City, preparing for his lieutenant's exam and courting Jane Renwick, whom he had known when both were children and whom Mammy Reed had predicted would become his bride. Despite the supposed toughness of the exam, competition from several other suitors for Jane's hand, and objections from her mother, he succeeded at both: He and Jane wed on April 26, 1826, just two days before his official promotion to lieutenant. In his autobiography, Wilkes stated that he scored the highest of all those examined, although the testers still had "very many yet to examine," and he expressed disappointment that the test did not include spherical trigonometry and algebra, depriving him of the opportunity to show what he "really knew." Examiner Lambert, Wilkes opined, "was not prepared to undertake

Among Wilkes's prominent English ancestors was his great-uncle John, caricatured here by the renowned English satirical artist William Hogarth. While he was a member of Parliament, John Wilkes's attack on King George III earned him arrest, imprisonment, and exile. A champion of the rights of the American colonies during the revolutionary war, he was later elected lord mayor of London. Wilkes strongly disapproved of his great-uncle, who was equally well known for his infamously dissolute way of life.

the examination in the higher branches . . . if he had ever studied them." He was more gracious concerning his spouse, whom he described as "a perfect lady in all her thoughts and expressions."

Most of the next several years were spent on leave, studying: geomagnetism with his brother-in-law James Renwick, a well-respected engineer and professor of natural philosophy at Columbia College; mathematics with Nathaniel Bowditch, America's foremost navigator and the prestigious author of the *New American Practical Navigator*, the bible of New World sea captains; surveying with Ferdinand Hassler, the first superintendent of the United States Coast Survey and a pioneer in the use of the new triangulation method of surveying. Although in comparison with these titans of the American scientific community Wilkes's achievements were modest to the point of nonexistence, he was one of the few officers in the navy to view himself as a scientist and virtually the only American

Young topmen—those entrusted with the management of the rigging of sails and ropes on a sailing ship—receive some on-the-job training. As a young sailor, Wilkes was appalled by the arbitrary and often tyrannical authority wielded by navy captains, but as a commander he would himself become notorious as a heavy-handed disciplinarian.

Wilkes married Jane Renwick, his childhood sweetheart, on April 26, 1826, just two days before he received his promotion to lieutenant. The Renwicks were a prominent and well-connected New York family who were able to aid Wilkes in promoting his career.

sailor to undergo such comprehensive training. He also gained additional practical experience, on a couple of short cruises and a survey of Narragansett Bay. His diligence led to his being named in 1833 superintendent of the Depot of Charts and Instruments (a forerunner of the Navy Oceanographic Office) in Washington, D.C. Although he proved to be a most able and energetic director, Wilkes had his eye on another position from the time he received his appointment. He wished to be given command of the proposed U.S. exploring expedition to the Pacific. Later, he wrote that he would have gladly given away his "old shoes & gone barefooted to have served on it," but his enthusiasm for the venture was not shared by everyone.

Taking Command

There were many reasons why proponents believed that the government of the United States should sponsor an exploratory expedition to the Pacific, but all arguments in favor of the venture basically fell into one of three interrelated (for purposes of the current discussion) categories— commerce, science, and national interest. By the late 1820s, large numbers of American ships were regularly plying the waters of the Pacific in search of whales (for their oil, used in lamps), seals (for their fur), sandalwood (coveted for making furniture and incense), and other resources. Even earlier, the English parliamentarian Edmund Burke had expressed dismay over the competition posed by the industrious American men of the sea: "[There is] no sea but what is vexed by their fisheries, no climate that is not witness of their toils." Supporters of a Pacific expedition argued that it would do much to bolster this burgeoning transoceanic commerce, at the least by obtaining reliable, up-to-date charts and maps of the Pacific, at the most by establishing U.S. bases in the region. In 1825, President John Quincy Adams argued that "a flourishing commerce and fishery extending to the islands of the Pacific and to China . . . require that the protecting power of the Union should be deployed under its flag as well upon the ocean as upon the land."

America's men of science agreed, if not for precisely the same reason. Inspired by the great exploratory expeditions of England's Captain James Cook, who between 1768 and

This sketch of two sailors at work was done by Agate, whose drawings, paintings, and engravings based upon his experiences during the South Seas Exploring Expedition make it appropriate, according to the historian William H. Goetzmann, that he be "ranked among the most important of early American artists."

Dr. John Cleves Symmes, the self-styled Newton of the West, as sketched by the famed American naturalist and painter John James Audubon. Among the Americans intrigued by Symmes's "holes-in-the poles" theory was Edgar Allan Poe, who made use of Symmes's ideas in his stories "MS. Found in a Bottle" and "A Descent into the Maelstrom" and the novella The Narrative of A. Gordon Pym.

1779, on three different voyages, circumnavigated the globe, explored Hawaii, Alaska, New Zealand, Australia, and reached as far south as any mariner had yet done; and by the Frenchman Comte Jean François de Galaup de la Pérouse, who explored the Pacific from Australia to the Bering Strait, America's intellectual community was eager to stake its own claim to scientific prominence. The Pacific, viewed as one of the world's last great unexplored regions, was acknowledged as the most prominent field for such endeavors. Since Cook's first voyage, England had manned 27 Pacific exploratory expeditions; France, 17; Russia, 7; Spain, 5; and Holland, 1. The ships of these nations regularly carried ethnologists, astronomers, cartographers, botanists, and artists to the myriad island chains of the Pacific, and they returned with their holds filled with exotic plant and animal specimens, sketches and watercolors of mysterious and enchanting new regions, and a wealth of scientific data. Tired of Europe's claims to scientific superiority, America's scientists wished to do as much.

And in this case, scientific achievement and national interest walked hand in hand. The great European expeditions were usually conducted under military auspices; while exploring, the navies of England and France often found time to make territorial claims as well. John Quincy Adams, who in his annual message to Congress in 1825 recommended the creation of an American exploring expedition, was among those who recognized that the acquisition of scientific knowledge in and of itself would contribute immeasurably to America's national prestige. Referring to the great European expeditions, he said, "The voyages of discovery prosecuted . . . at the expense of those nations have not only redounded to their glory, but to the improvement of human knowledge. We have been partakers of that improvement and owe for it a sacred debt not only of gratitude, but of equal and proportional exertion in the same common cause." He went on to point out that "one hundred expeditions of circumnavigation like those of Cook and La Pérouse would not burden the exchequer [treasury] of the nation . . . so much as the ways and means of defraying a single campaign in war" and, one may infer, would serve America's global interests and ambitions equally as well.

Much of the scientific interest in the South Seas concerned the existence and character (if indeed it existed) of Antarctica. Was there a land mass, a continent, beneath the ice that covered the southern polar regions? Cook's and subsequent voyages had left the issue unresolved. By the end of the 1820s, the British Admiralty, the government department responsible for the navy and maritime endeavors, had declared that the question of the existence of a continent at the southern pole was one of the few remaining geographic mysteries. In the United States speculation about the nature of Terra Australis Incognita, as the purported southern land mass was often referred to, took a curious turn, owing to an unusual theory offered by one John Cleves Symmes, a self-taught former soldier from Cincinnati, Ohio, who styled himself the "Newton of the West," and the tireless promotional efforts of Jeremiah Reynolds, an Ohio newspaper editor and would-be explorer.

In 1818, Symmes had hypothesized that the earth was hollow and that beyond the icy barriers at the poles there existed a warmer climate and entries to the earth's center. Ships that were able to conquer the ice would thus find a "warm and rich land, stocked with thrifty vegetables and animals, if not men" from where they would be able to sail into the earth's core, which was "hollow and habitable." He won many supporters, among them Reynolds and a host of whaling merchants, and carried his theories to the public by means of a series of lectures, during which he illustrated his point by use of a specially constructed

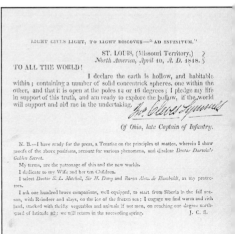

Symmes had this announcement published on April 10, 1818, and subsequently sent a copy to John Quincy Adams, then the secretary of state. It declared that "the earth is hollow, and habitable within" and asked for 100 "brave companions" to accompany him on an expedition northward from Siberia with reindeer and sleighs to prove the contention.

globe and called for a government expedition to prove his contentions. By 1825, 9 petitions had been sent to Congress urging that body to fund an expedition, and 50 Pennsylvania legislators urged the federal government to equip the expedition on the grounds that Symmes's theory was "quite as reasonable as that of the great Columbus [and] better supported by the facts." Not all those who backed Symmes's call for a South Seas expedition necessarily supported his holes in the poles theory, however. Sea captains, for example, were more interested in learning of new whaling and sealing grounds than sailing to the center of the earth, and many scientists supported the expedition in the certainty that it would debunk, rather than prove, Symmes's fanciful notions. Even Reynolds eventually backed away from Symmes's theories, but his support for an exploratory expedition grew no less ardent. He devoted

This 1838 lithograph mocks the proposed U.S. exploring expedition. In one segment, at upper left, the artist, who satirically signed himself Robinson Crusoe, portrays an expedition reduced by government penury to a single rowboat oared through an Antarctic seascape by a convict conscript while a pompous admiral gives directions, a gentleman scientist peers through a telescope, and a bohemian artist sketches.

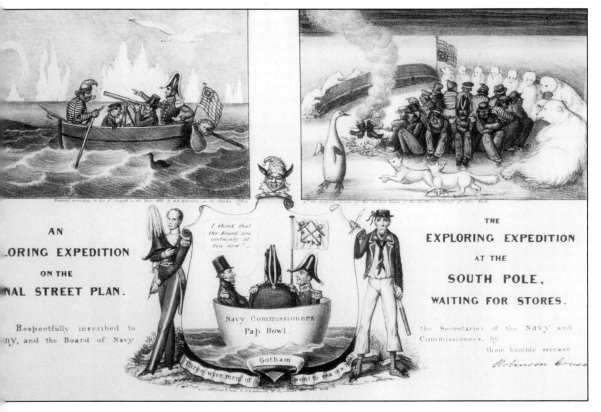

himself to gathering as much information as could be obtained from written accounts of nautical voyages and from personal interviews with the captains of whaling and trading vessels who had visited the Pacific, and he worked untiringly to keep the cause of a South Seas expedition alive, cultivating friends and acquaintances as disparate as the secretary of the navy and the great writer of the macabre Edgar Allan Poe, arguing the needs of commerce, science, and national interest. In 1828, he was asked to present his case before Congress; later that year, Congress passed preliminary legislation for an expedition and authorized the construction of a single ship to carry it out. The *Peacock*, a 559-ton sloop-of-war, was launched at the New York navy yard in September, but the following February southern senators blocked the passage of necessary further appropriations on the grounds that the money could be better spent at home.

For eight years the expedition remained nothing more than a subject for continual debate and public squabbling. Reynolds went to sea with a privately sponsored South Seas expedition, but his voyage only honed his enthusiasm, and after his return in 1834 he renewed his lobbying efforts for a government-sponsored venture. Others had grown tired of the subject. Congressional opponents sarcastically referred to the South Sea bubble, and one newspaper regularly and scornfully called it the "Deplorable Expedition." Even Adams, now a member of the House of Representatives and formerly a steadfast supporter, quipped that the only thing he "wanted to hear about the exploring expedition was that it had sailed."

At last, in 1836, Congress authorized the expenditure of $150,000 for the United States South Seas Exploring Expedition. The enterprise was to be directed by the secretary of the navy, Mahlon Dickerson; he in turn appointed Commodore Thomas ap Catesby Jones as commander. Jones had plenty of experience in the South Seas—he had been commander of the small U.S. Pacific squadron between 1826 and 1831, during which time he had been the first U.S. naval officer to call at Tahiti and had also concluded a treaty with King Kamehameha III of Hawaii—but he was unprepared for the heightened infighting and dissension that accompanied the preparations for the expedition. Arguments raged over everything from the size and type of the ships to be used to the composition of the crews, and Jones was caught in the middle of every one, most importantly the battle between the navy and the "scientifics." As an old sea dog, Jones was skeptical of scientists and believed that the navy was fully capable by itself of carrying out the mission, but Reynolds and his many congressional and public supporters wanted a full complement of scientists to sail with the expedition. Dickerson, whose motto was "be cautious not to attempt too much business in one day," left the responsibility up to Jones, who was extremely uncomfortable, to say the least, in the crossfire.

Most of Jones's decisions reflected his confusion—for example, the *Macedonian*, his designated flagship, the largest ship in the navy, was too big to take necessary coastline soundings—but he did have the wisdom to send one Lieutenant Charles Wilkes to England to purchase the necessary scientific supplies for the expedition. (Wilkes's selection may in fact have owed more to the intense politicking surrounding the expedition than to Jones's foresight: The suggestion that he be named was apparently made to Jones by a member of the politically powerful Renwick family, into which Wilkes had married.) By the time Wilkes returned from England in January 1837 with, according to historian William H. Goetzmann, "the largest collection of scientific instruments and foreign charts ever assembled in the United States," Jones's unsuitability for the task confronting him had become apparent even to himself. Spying an opportunity, Wilkes turned down several appointments—as a civilian astronomer and as commander of one of the exploratory vessels— to the expedition that he later professed he would have

Midshipman William Reynolds, a well-born member of the expedition seen here in a sketch by an unknown artist, initially admired its commander, but in their entirety his letters and journal constitute a revealing (and deflating) counterpoint to Wilkes's self-serving narratives.

gone barefoot to have served on. Jones failed to last out the year; citing ill health, he resigned in December 1837, and after several interim appointments proved unworthy, Wilkes was offered command on March 20, 1838. After receiving assurances that he would have total control over all aspects of the expedition, he accepted.

His appointment ignited a fire storm of controversy. Although Wilkes was now 40, and Jones, for example, had been just 35 when he took command of the Pacific squadron, many of Wilkes's fellow officers believed that he was too young to command even a single ship, let alone an entire expedition. More to the point was that 38 of the navy's 40 lieutenants had more experience than did Wilkes. In addition, his scientific accomplishments made him somewhat suspect in the eyes of those who considered themselves "regular" navy; at least one senior officer viewed his scientific interests as "peculiar." Wilkes was

One of the 19th century's most eminent men of science, James Dwight Dana was the greatest of the scientifics who served with the South Seas Exploring Expedition. Dana was 25 when he shipped out and had already made a name for himself as a promising mineralogist; his work on the expedition earned him a reputation as a world-class geologist.

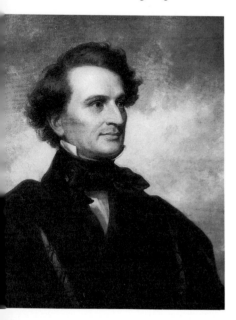

accused, with some accuracy, of shamelessly campaigning for his position, behavior that though commonplace was considered bad form, especially by those bypassed. In a letter to her husband, Jane Wilkes described Washington as "in a blaze" over his selection; a naval lieutenant stationed in Norfolk, Virginia, described other officers as being "all up in arms about the appointment."

Beleaguered, Wilkes compelled the new secretary of war, Joel Roberts Poinsett, to issue a statement to the effect that he had not attempted to further his own career at the expense of his brother officers, but in other ways he demonstrated an imperious, characteristic disregard for what was thought of him. In naming his officers, Wilkes overlooked many who were supremely qualified in terms of experience and ability. The result was an extremely youthful officer corps. William Reynolds (no relation to Jeremiah), a 22-year-old midshipman whose journal—kept from Wilkes's prying eyes—and letters to his family constitute a fascinating chronicle of the expedition, found it strange to "find none but youthful faces among the officers—a Young Captain, with boys for his subordinates—no gray hairs among us." Wilkes's stated reasons for selecting such a youthful crew were that younger sailors would be less tempted by debauchery in foreign ports—the lieutenant was a stern moralist—and that they would be more likely than older officers to recall the scientific and mathematical material they had mastered for their officers' exams, making them more valuable in carrying out scientific duties. He probably also believed that younger officers would have less reason to resent his command and would therefore be less likely to challenge him.

Wilkes had similarly strong feelings about the civilian contingent, the so-called scientifics. Although Wilkes's scientific background, which gave him a presumed ability to deal with the "scientific question," was the single most important reason for his appointment as commander, once

in charge he demonstrated a jealousy of the military's pre-
rogatives that would have satisfied even the most regular
of navy men. He made it preeminently clear that the
United States South Seas Exploring Expedition was to be
first and foremost a navy operation. The expedition's official instructions, which Wilkes wrote for Dickerson's approval, emphasized that its primary mission was to be the
preparation of navigational charts, the one scientific task
for which the navy was well suited. Fearing that the scientifics, in their quest for botanical and biological specimens, would relegate the navy officers to "mere hewers
of wood and drawers of water," Wilkes relentlessly whittled
the number of civilian expedition members from the 25
proposed by Reynolds to a mere 9, and 2 more would be
dismissed in the course of the voyage. James Dwight Dana,
who already enjoyed a considerable reputation as a mineralogist, would prove to be the most gifted of the group;
the philologist Horatio Hale, whose work in many ways
anticipated the concerns and methods of modern ethnol-
ogy, and the naturalist Charles Pickering also distinguished
themselves. Two artists, Alfred T. Agate and Joseph Drayton, were also numbered among the scientifics. Perhaps
the most well known American scientist of the day, the
botanist Asa Gray, was originally slated to be a member
of the expedition, but at the last moment he resigned in
order to fill the first professorship of botany ever created
in the United States. It is likely that the conflict between
the military and the scientifics, which Gray foresaw con-
tinuing throughout the course of the expedition, also influenced his decision.

In taking a hard line on the scientific question, Wilkes
was guarding his own interests as well as the prestige of
the navy. The lieutenant placed himself in charge of all
matters pertaining to physics, surveying, astronomy, mag-
netism, and geodesy and declared that these would be the
most important areas of the expedition's inquiries. Finally,

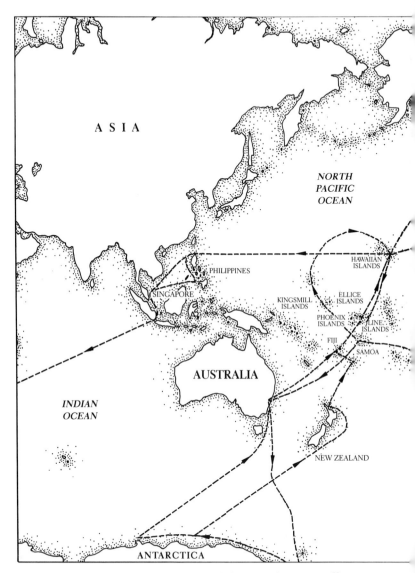

intending to pen his own account of the expedition, Wilkes callously dismissed Jeremiah Reynolds, who had been intending to sail as the expedition's historian, having been appointed to that post several years earlier by President Andrew Jackson. The dismissal came on August 13, just 5 days before the 6 ships of the United States South Seas Exploring Expedition, manned by 346 hands—the flag-

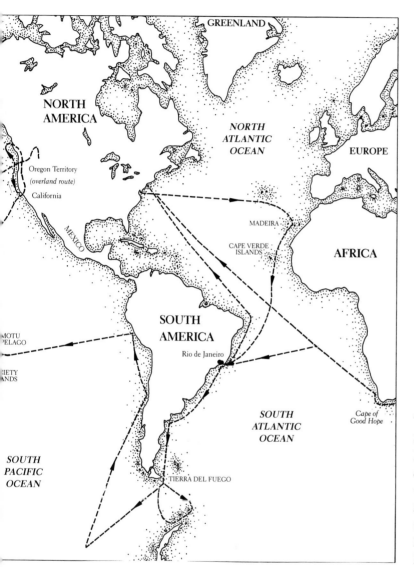

The route taken by the United States South Seas Exploring Expedition, the last such expedition to circumnavigate the world in sailing ships. The South Seas Exploring Expedition is also referred to as the Exploring Expedition or the Wilkes Expedition.

ship *Vincennes* and the man-of-war *Peacock*, the supply ship *Relief*, the brig *Porpoise*, and the schooners *Flying Fish* and *Sea Gull*—set sail from Hampton Roads, Virginia. The harbor pilot who guided the fleet out to sea observed that he had never seen men "more bent on accomplishing all within their power for the honor and glory of the navy and of the country, and full of life and zeal."

The Silver Sea

The squadron initially followed an easterly course across the Atlantic to the island of Madeira (some 350 miles off the coast of Morocco) and then to the Cape Verde Islands (about 300 miles west of Senegal and 1,500 miles southwest of Madeira), where the ships took on supplies and the scientifics had their first opportunity to engage in the onshore collection of specimens. En route, captain and crew got to know their vessels. Wilkes learned that the heavily laden supply ship *Relief* was too slow to keep up with the remainder of the fleet, so he ordered it ahead to Rio de Janeiro, Brazil, the next scheduled stop. He also learned that the *Peacock*, commanded by his most trustworthy officer, William Hudson, was barely seaworthy. Plans were made for extensive repairs at Rio.

The men of the South Seas Exploring Expedition also got to know the character of their commander. Initially, they were optimistic, buoyed by Wilkes's decisiveness and energy in finally getting the expedition to sea. What the blundering Jones had been unable to do in a couple of years, Wilkes had achieved in just a few months. As one officer put it, the crew was "ready to believe that [Wilkes] must be the very beau ideal of a Captain for the hazardous Enterprise in which they had embarked." Reynolds described him as a man "of great talent, perhaps genius." The meticulous attention to detail that would characterize his command for the next four years was soon in evidence.

Agate's drawing formed the basis for this engraving of a native of Patagonia, which appeared in Wilkes's narratives. Wilkes and his men apparently sighted none of the giants that earlier explorers reported encountering along the windswept, desolate coastline of Patagonia, the southernmost region of present-day Argentina.

On the voyage from the Cape Verdes to Rio de Janeiro, Wilkes insisted upon daily inspections during which each crew in turn lined up on the deck of its vessel while he scrutinized them through his spyglass. Each day, in addition to their normal duties, officers were required to take hourly readings of the air temperature at the masthead and on deck, measure water temperature both on and below the surface, and determine the direction and force of water currents. When doing so would not interfere with their normal duties, officers were to aid the scientists in capturing plant and animal specimens from the sea. The crew's confidence in its commander soon turned to unease, however. At least one member had served with Wilkes before, and that experience had been so painful and humiliating that he had vowed vengeance. Less than two weeks out, on the night of August 29, a young sailor named Charles Erskine crept to the skylight above Wilkes's stateroom, planning to drop through and bludgeon the lieutenant to death with an iron belaying pin. On an earlier voyage under Wilkes, Erskine had been stretched over a gun and flogged mercilessly with a knotted rope (called by sailors a colt) because he made the mistake of getting some letters wet while retrieving mail from another ship. According to his own account of his life at sea, *Twenty Years Before the Mast*, Erskine was persuaded to desist from his murderous plan when he saw a vision of his mother's face.

Wilkes had undergone no such transformation. He held himself apart from officers and crew, usually dined alone, and prized himself on being a stern taskmaster in the belief that "there is nothing like a proper discipline enjoined and kept up by all as tending to harmony of action and Strict obedience to orders." When a lookout on the *Vincennes* fell asleep on duty, Wilkes imposed the maximum punishment allowed by naval regulations—a dozen strokes with the cat-o'-nine-tails. Later on in the voyage, the lieutenant would not be so merciful: On several occasions he applied as many as 40 lashes. He took pains to cultivate

the reputation of a "martinet" because "once established [it] goes far to carry with it authority and induce obedience to command, and I knew that the example of the Flagship would govern the Rest of the Squadron."

The scientifics as well as the crew suffered poor relations with the expedition's commander, who seemed to go out of his way to make things difficult for them. On calm days they dragged huge scoop nets through the water, emptied their contents upon the ship's deck, and sifted through their finds, often discovering, according to Reynolds, "the most minute and beautiful [things] to look at." Little realizing that what were "trifles" to the untrained eye were often fascinating aquatic life-forms, Reynolds was astounded at the "patient manner in which they toil, toil, seemingly for trifles, giving up their whole soul to their employment." The more notable specimens were immediately turned over to the artists for sketching. Watching the artists at work, wrote the appreciative Reynolds, was "another source of gratification."

A contemplative young sailor, as drawn by Agate. It was not uncommon for boys in their early teens to serve in the American and British navies of the day, and even the officers of the Exploring Expedition were notable for their youth. Tars or jacks, as sailors were often referred to, often did not wear shoes while performing their duties because leather soles tended to slip on wet decks and rigging.

But the patience of the scientifics would be sorely tried by a Wilkes edict that forbade them from bringing their specimens below deck and particularly to their living quarters, which on the average measured six by seven and one-half feet and were described by Reynolds as being filled with "dead & living lizards, & fish floating in alcohol, and sharks jaws, & stuffed turtles, and vertebraes and Animalculae frisking in jars of salt water, and old shells, and many other equally interesting pieces of furniture hanging about their beds." (Reynolds was no doubt taken by the contrast between the scientifics' cubbyholes and his more lavishly appointed cabin, which he and his roommate had decorated with white-and-crimson curtains, blue damask–covered couches, plated candlesticks, a Brussels carpet, and bowie knives, cutlasses, and pistols that gave a "Man-of-War finish to the whole.") The lieutenant was annoyed by the stench emanating from below decks and feared that the specimens could somehow spread disease, and he turned a deaf ear to the scientifics' protest that they

Charles Sands, a clerk to Captain Cadwalader Ringgold of the Porpoise, sketched in his journal this scene of a sailor being flogged. At the time, corporal discipline aboard ships was commonplace, but Wilkes's fondness for ordering the cat-o'-nine-tails well laid on was considered to be beyond the pale by many of those who served under him.

had nowhere else to work on their finds. According to Titian Peale, the scion of a famous Philadelphia scientific and artistic family who had shipped with the expedition as a naturalist, the problem was more than just Wilkes's intransigence. Peale regarded the ships as completely inadequate for scientific work; the only suitable space for the scientifics' labor, he believed, was Wilkes's cabin.

As previously, the scientifics had reason to believe that self-interest influenced Wilkes's decisions. All specimens were to be placed in the charge of the officer of the deck, meaning that they were, indirectly at least, in Wilkes's control. Later, the lieutenant grew more explicit. Everything collected during the voyage was government property, Wilkes informed the men of the expedition, and must be surrendered to him; there would be no exceptions. He also ordered every officer to keep a journal in which was to be recorded "all objects of interest however small which may take place during the cruise," and he reviewed these journals weekly. The reasoning behind such orders became apparent in time; Wilkes intended to control every aspect of the publication of accounts and findings related to the expedition. (Wilkes's later narratives of the expeditions made liberal use of direct quotations from these sources without attribution.) In a letter to Gray, Dana congratulated him on escaping "Naval servitude" by remaining at home.

As Wilkes had proved earlier in his career, he was not unfavorably disposed to science, but he did wish to ensure that the scientific achievements of the expedition were credited as much as possible to the navy and to himself. In Rio de Janeiro, where the fleet arrived in late November, he demonstrated again his dedication to scientific inquiry and reinforced his image as a humorless tyrant. Two officers and a member of the crew of the *Peacock* spent an entire day climbing formidable Sugarloaf Mountain, which towers over Rio's harbor, but instead of earning their commander's approval for the feat—they were the first Americans to scale the peak—they reaped his scorn. In a terse note to Hudson, Wilkes wrote that he had learned with "surprise & regret that an officer of your ship made an excursion to an important height in this vicinity without obtaining the necessary instruments for its correct admeasurement"; the officers should be made to duplicate their feat, this time with the proper scientific equipment, lest it result "only in the idle & boastful saying that its summit has been reached, instead of [in] an excursion which might have been useful to the expedition." The two officers gamely returned to the peak and measured the mountain's height, but this time they spent the night on the summit and built a large bonfire that, according to Reynolds, "brought all Rio out in wonder to see."

Reynolds was charged with scientific duties of his own. After Wilkes established an observatory on an island at the harbor's mouth, Reynolds was assigned the unenviable task of recording its instrument readings, which required that he be roused by a marine guard every hour. While the scientifics gathered specimens ashore, Hudson oversaw repairs to the hull, spars, and masts of the *Peacock*, which had been, in Wilkes's words, "in a wretched state to go to sea."

With the *Relief* having once more been sent on ahead, the remaining five ships departed Rio de Janeiro on January 6, 1839. After several weeks spent on surveying work near the mouth of the Rio Negro in Argentina, where the dispute between the scientifics and Wilkes intensified following an incident in which officers of the *Sea Gull* refused to retrieve a shore party numbering Peale among its members, Wilkes ordered the squadron to set sail for Orange Harbor on Hoste, an island 85 miles northwest of Cape Horn, South America's southernmost point. "The safest harbour on the coast," according to Wilkes, who remained extremely secretive about his plans throughout the course of the entire voyage, it was to serve as the base from which the expedition embarked upon its first polar voyage.

Eerie environmental phenomena manifested themselves as the fleet sailed south and the weather grew colder. On January 19, the ships encountered patches of water colored from a species of salpa, a small jellyfishlike animal. Wilkes noted that "the sea became very luminous, the vessels in passing through the water leaving long bright trains behind them." By 10:00 P.M. this smooth "sea of silver," coupled with lightning to the west, an enveloping haze, and a mysterious 10-degree drop in air and water temperature produced a most "mysterious and alarming sensation." Wilkes speculated that the remarkable fall in temperature resulted from "the near approach to icebergs," even though the fleet was still far north of the polar regions. Further marvels awaited. Off the high, rugged coast of

Tierra del Fuego, a parhelion—2 illusory suns on the horizon alongside the real one—appeared for 15 minutes on the morning of February 16. That night, Captain Cadwalader Ringgold of the *Porpoise* captured a large medusa, or jellyfish, nine feet in circumference, with tentacles seven feet long. The next day, more mirages caused single ships to appear as three images—two upright and one inverted. The coastline also appeared distorted. At Orange Harbor, Wilkes readied the expedition for its assault on the polar seas. "Exploring clothing," consisting of poor-quality pea jackets and boots, was issued to each crew member. The boots, one sarcastic surgeon observed, operated on the "sieve principle"; frigid water gushed out as quickly as it had entered, and the men resorted to wrapping their feet in blankets. More devastating to morale was Wilkes's decision—motivated by his constant and unfounded suspicions that a "mutinous cabal" was at work against him—to rework his command structure by transferring officers among ships, with little or no regard for seniority or ability. Two blameless lieutenants were exiled to the *Relief*, which would not be making the voyage to Antarctica, as were all of the scientifics with the exception of Peale. The *Vincennes* was also ordered to stay behind, for the purpose of establishing an observatory at Orange Harbor and doing surveying work along Tierra del Fuego.

Wilkes divided the remaining four ships in hopes of improving the chances of a significant discovery. He ordered the *Peacock* and the *Flying Fish*, under Hudson's command, to sail southwest in an attempt to surpass Cook's famous "Ne Plus Ultra" (the point at which the ice barrier stopped the famous explorer in 1774, the southernmost latitude yet attained). Wilkes's own vessel, the *Porpoise*, and the *Sea Gull* would proceed south to explore the southeast side of Palmer's Land (the Antarctic Peninsula) and beyond. At 7:00 A.M. on February 25, the *Porpoise* and *Sea Gull* weighed anchor; Wilkes later wrote that when Hudson and the other officers took their leave at the mouth of the harbor, "I felt greatly depressed, for I was well aware that we had many, very many dangers to encounter before meeting again."

A few days out of Orange Harbor, the men of the *Porpoise* saw their first icebergs. Wilkes marveled at the sight, apparently unconcerned with the dangers they posed to even the sturdiest ship. "I have rarely seen a finer sight," he wrote in his narrative of the journey. "The sea was literally studded with these beautiful masses, some of pure white, others showing all the shades of the opal, others emerald green, and occasionally here and there some of a deep black." As the ships sailed on in almost perpetual daylight, cape pigeons and the gray-and-black petrel appeared frequently, albatrosses hovered about, and penguins, sometimes encircling the ships, uttered "their discordant screams."

Joseph Couthouy, the expedition's conchologist (one who specializes in the branch of zoology concerned with the study of shells), did this sketch of the huge jellyfish captured by Captain Ringgold of the Porpoise *near Cape Horn in the early morning hours of February 17, 1839.*

Near Palmer's Land on March 3, the men counted 80 large icebergs. Sailing so close together in the constant fog and mist as to pose a danger to one another, the *Porpoise* and *Sea Gull* pressed on through a sea covered with massive ice islands, just one of which could easily have caved in their hull. By March 5, ice had encased the riggings and covered the decks, making sailing all but impossible. Most of the men were suffering from exposure, and a few were afflicted with scurvy. With any approach to Palmer's Land barred by the ice and accurate depth and sound readings out of the question, Wilkes decided that the "season for such explorations had gone by" and ordered his ships to turn back.

The return trip was no less daunting. Gales forced the *Porpoise* to seek shelter in Good Success Bay, in the South Shetland Islands, where a small party commanded by Lieutenant John Dale succeeded in sailing a launch through the heavy surf and reaching the shore. But increasingly poor weather prevented their return to the *Porpoise* for several days, and when a second boat was sent ashore with provisions, it capsized in the storm-tossed waves, fortunately without loss of life.

The fleet of the South Seas Exploring Expedition lies at anchor in Orange Harbor on February 22, 1839. This sketch by Lieutenant George Emmons of the expedition illustrates the relative size of the ships. The Porpoise *is at far right, the* Peacock, Vincennes, *and* Relief, *top to bottom, are at center, and the* Flying Fish *and* Sea Gull *are at left.*

The *Porpoise* returned to Orange Harbor on March 30, eight days after the *Sea Gull*, which had itself ridden out "extremely unfavorable" weather, anchored off Deception Island in the South Shetlands. Shore parties there discovered that penguins, covering "some hundreds of acres," resented their intrusion and sometimes "seized the aggressor with their bill, and beat him with their flipper," according to Wilkes. The officers thought the penguins' bearing "quite courageous, and their retreat dignified, as far as their ridiculous waddle would permit."

Farther westward, the *Peacock* and the *Flying Fish* had no shortage of adventure. Within two days of leaving Orange Harbor, they lost track of one another; it was not until March 25 that they were reunited. By that point, Hudson, aboard the *Peacock*, had with good cause decided to turn back. "No vessel," Wilkes maintained, could have been "more uncomfortable than the *Peacock*," even after the repairs performed on it at Rio de Janeiro. Its gunports were so defective that even when covered with double tarpaulins (sheets of canvas waterproofed with either tar or paint) they failed to shut out the sea. As a result, the gun deck was constantly wet—Peale was forced to abandon his cabin there—and the ship was damp throughout. The bow and gun deck were not sealed watertight until the "Antarctic Caulker" covered it with ice. The shoddy exploring clothing worn by the men offered as little protection and, by Wilkes's estimate, contributed to at least one death: On March 9, a sailor plunged from the topsails into the turbulent sea. He was rescued, only to die the next day from his injuries. Wilkes blamed his fall on the defective boots the expedition had been issued. Despite these hindrances, Hudson and the *Peacock* managed to reach 68 degrees 8 minutes south latitude, nearly 5 degrees farther south than Wilkes had attained, before the "dictates of common prudence," in Peale's words, forced them to head north, to Valparaiso, Chile, where the necessary repairs could be made.

The *Flying Fish*'s voyage was the most successful and the most harrowing of all. Gale winds split the ship's jib and mainsail; once, a whale surfaced and rubbed its sides against the battered vessel. By late March, according to James C. Palmer, the ship's doctor, icebergs surrounded the vessel "like tombs in some vast cemetery," and hoarfrost covered the men until "they looked like spectres fit for such a haunt." (Lieutenant William Walker, the ship's commander, was familiar with sepulchral imagery; before leaving Orange Harbor he had been genially assured by some of his colleagues that the tiny *Flying Fish* "would make him an honorable coffin.") According to the physician, "The eye ached for some limit to a space which the mind could hardly grasp. Mountain against mountain blended with a sky whose very whiteness was horrible. All things were the same chilling hue." Despite a warning from the ship's carpenter that the vessel could not stand the strain, on March 25 the *Flying Fish* rammed its way south through "sutures" in the ice, only to be trapped again two days later. Palmer observed that "many an eye wandered over the hapless vessel, to estimate how long she might last for fuel" while the ship attempted to batter its way through the encircling ice. Finally, after reaching open sea, Walker decided to head north. The little schooner and its plucky crew had reached almost 70 degrees south latitude, about one degree short of Cook's Ne Plus Ultra.

In its presumably safer harbor, the *Relief* and its crew fared little better than the polar explorers. While surveying the Strait of Magellan, the supply ship was bombarded by several violent gales. During one particularly fierce storm near Noir Island, the sea "broke tremendously" against a reef, and the *Relief*'s anchor cables dragged across the rocky bottom as the ship was swept ever closer to the reef and destruction. The cables, George Sinclair remembered, made "the most awful sound I ever heard and the Lord grant I may never hear it again." The ship pitched "as if

half mad: her decks deluged with the sweeping waves, which poured in torrents down the hatches." At the last moment, the wind shifted, and the vessel cleared the reef. Its commanding officer, acting on what he believed were Wilkes's implicit orders, immediately took the *Relief* to the more hospitable waters of Valparaiso.

The crew of the *Vincennes* encountered similar difficulties but underwent some singular experiences as well. In its 2 months at Orange Harbor, it endured 11 gales, during which, according to Reynolds, "blasts" of wind blew with "such tremendous fury that it seemed to me as if the Ship would be lifted out of the water and borne away." In this same period, the crew also became the first

The Flying Fish *tests its fragile frame against the ice as it nears Captain James Cook's famous "Ne Plus Ultra" on the first Antarctic voyage of the Exploring Expedition. The painting is by Peale from a sketch by Lieutenant William Walker, who was then in command of the schooner. "I would not have believed a ship could pass through such dangers,"* Walker wrote.

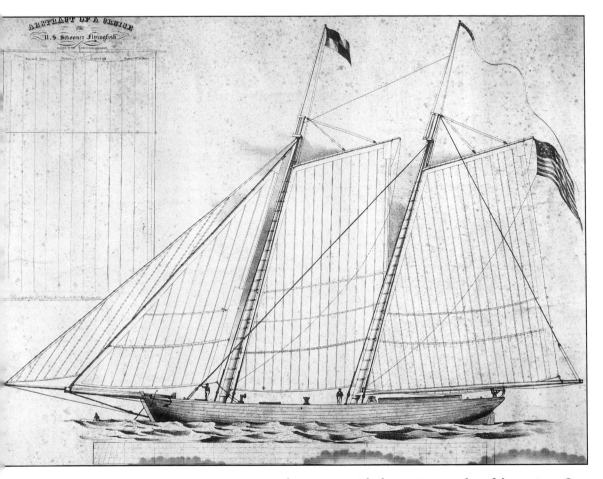

ABSTRACT OF A CRUISE
of the
U. S. Schooner Flyingfish

The Flying Fish *was a 96-ton schooner armed with 2 small cannons and manned by a crew of 15. As the* Independence, *it had previously served as a pilot boat in New York harbor. It was the smallest of Wilkes's six original ships, none of which performed more nobly.*

to make contact with the native peoples of the region. One morning in March, three small canoes appeared alongside the massive flagship. In each, an Indian family sat around a small fire that burned on a mound of sand and stones. The timid Fuegians traded their fish spears—10 feet long and tipped with a whale-tooth head—for such trinkets as buttons and red flannel, which had been brought along for just such contingencies. To his amazement, one officer soon discovered that the Indians were excellent mimics. He took one Indian man by the arm and, while singing a tune, waltzed him around the deck. The native followed perfectly. When one of the artists played a few notes on his violin, the Indians carefully imitated the sound. For the most part, however, the sailors found the Indians repulsive. Reynolds scorned the Indians for their seeming wretchedness, overlooking completely their ability to survive in an environment that the Americans, with all their technical sophistication, found extremely challenging. The Indians, he wrote, were "the most hideously ugly race in the world, go naked entirely, even in the snow storms, smear themselves with filth and nastiness, eat revolting food, have scarcely the instinct of a brute and are certainly destitute of the human quality of reason."

Perhaps Reynolds's judgment was affected by his eagerness for the expedition to move on to warmer climes, for later on, after many more encounters with native peoples, he would demonstrate a much less ethnocentric cast of mind in lamenting the "black train of consequences" unleashed by western contact with the aboriginal inhabitants of the Pacific. Certainly, his letters reveal a man eager for a change of scenery—"You cannot conceive how wretchedly depressed and worn out we all became from tarrying so long in the cold, wet and stormy climate of T[i]erra del Fuego"—a sentiment shared by many of his comrades of the South Seas Exploring Expedition.

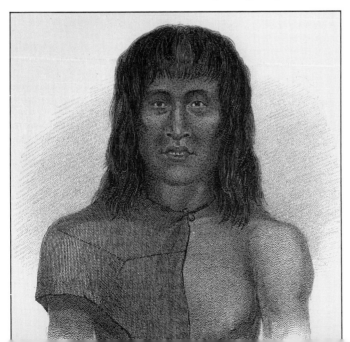

A native of Tierra del Fuego, from Wilkes's narratives. The men of the Exploring Expedition regarded the Fuegians, inhabitants of one of the most forbidding regions of the globe, as poor, primitive, and filthy. Among the Fuegian artifacts the scientifics collected were sealskin quivers, bows, arrows, and fish spears.

A False and Malignant Villain

In vivid contrast to Orange Harbor, the attractions of Valparaiso, where most of the squadron was safely anchored by May 15, included "a smiling sky, a mild climate, a Roadstead crowded with Ships of all nations, a busy town, and the lovely women," according to one admiring expedition officer. Wilkes immediately ordered an observatory established, and the scientifics embarked on collecting excursions to the countryside. Although most of the men found Valparaiso a welcome respite, the lieutenant hoped to avoid "all unnecessary delay" there, for the expedition was now several weeks behind schedule.

Also behind schedule was the *Sea Gull*, which with the *Flying Fish* had been designated by Wilkes to linger at Orange Harbor in hopes of finding the *Relief*, which the commander was unaware had gone on to Valparaiso ahead of the rest of the fleet. The *Flying Fish* finally arrived on May 19, alone, having lost track of its sister schooner during a frightening tempest. Wilkes, citing the stiff opposing winds between Valparaiso and Orange Harbor, professed not to find the delay extraordinary, but Reynolds, for one, feared the worst. "God help them and keep them from so terrible a death! It requires but little effort on my imagination to picture all its horrors," he wrote. His prayers were to no avail; the *Sea Gull*, with 15 hands aboard, had gone down somewhere between Orange Harbor and Valparaiso.

Malietoa, a Samoan native. Like many European explorers before them, the men of the U.S. Exploring Expedition found much to admire about the peoples and cultures of the Pacific Islands.

Agate's engraving of the gateway to Lima, Peru, which the expedition visited in the summer of 1839. Chilean troops, the victors in a recently concluded war between their nation and Peru, roamed the city while the explorers were there, and according to one sailor the six-mile road between Lima and its seaport at Callao "was infested by robbers who make their demands in open day without ceremony."

The schooner's absence gave Wilkes the opportunity to remove one of his least favorite officers, a Lieutenant Craven, whom he had previously accused of the grievous sin of joining in shipboard "merrymaking." When the squadron left Valparaiso in early June for Callao, which functioned as the seaport for Lima, Peru, Wilkes ordered the unfortunate lieutenant to stay behind, ostensibly to command the *Sea Gull* when it arrived. The commander, whose boorish interactions with foreign dignitaries and U.S. government officials in Brazil had already embarrassed his sailors, further disgraced himself by twice crashing the *Vincennes* into the *Peacock* as the fleet left the harbor, then running the flagship into a Danish vessel. Reynolds attributed the mishaps to Wilkes's "mismanagement and obstinacy"; the accidents put an end to whatever respect the men of the expedition harbored for their commander's seamanship.

Wilkes intended for the expedition to stop in Callao only long enough to "refit, replenish [its] stores and complete [its] duties." His wishes, for once, were fine with his crew, who found the seaport and surrounding areas filthy, ridden with thieves, and verging on anarchy. Reynolds was again assigned observatory duty, which he fulfilled alone in an isolated area he termed "the most cut-throat spot of the most villainous portion of the globe." There, the nervous midshipman barricaded his tent with a table and kept a "huge" sword in his lap and two pistols at close hand, but he was unmolested by the region's notorious bandits.

More than the dangerous surroundings adversely affected the morale of the expedition at Callao, for Wilkes continued his hard-driving ways. After several sailors raided the *Relief*'s whiskey casks—grog was routinely issued on long voyages—and became uproariously drunk, Wilkes, without convening a court-martial, felt "compelled" to dictate a "proper" punishment of 24 lashes to the offenders. The tipplers' behavior had been an intolerable breach of discipline, but Wilkes's response far exceeded what was customary. At the same time, he sentenced 2 deserters to 36 and 41 lashes, again far in excess of naval regulations. He also continued his practice of shuffling command, most damagingly by promoting a friend's nephew over older and more qualified candidates. According to Reynolds, the men of the expedition "all understand the motives that led to [the promotion] too well to admire them." After a court of inquiry rejected Wilkes's contention that Lieutenant Dale should be punished for failing to return to the *Porpoise* during the gale that had trapped him and his landing party in Good Success Bay, the commander simply transferred Dale, his friends, and other alleged troublemakers to the *Relief*, then ordered the supply ship home, charging that it was "ill-adapted to the service" and "retarded" operations.

On July 18, five days out from Callao heading west, Wilkes sprung a new surprise. He appeared on deck in a captain's uniform, which he had packed away in his seaman's trunk, and declared that he had, on his own authority, promoted himself (and Hudson) to captain, the rank that he believed, as squadron commander, he should rightfully possess. Wilkes asserted that only he knew the reason for the timing of his self-promotion, but observers, then and since, suspected that he waited until the fleet had set out across the vast Pacific because he knew that it was unlikely to encounter other navy vessels there.

At an average speed of about 130 miles a day, it took the fleet until August 13 to reach Clermont-Tonnerre Island (known today as Reao), one of the easternmost of the Tuamotu Archipelago. This tiny atoll—10 miles long by 1.5 miles wide—was in many ways typical of the hundreds of Pacific islands the expedition visited, surveyed, and charted. Its low, narrow white beaches, fringed, according to Reynolds, with "a dense growth of beautiful trees and shrubbery," encircled a lagoon "of a blue as transparent as the azure vault of Heaven"; the overall effect was "absolutely enchanting." Here, Wilkes unveiled the methods that would be standard operating procedure throughout much of the rest of the journey. The primary focus, as the orders Wilkes had written for himself had made clear, was to be surveying: that is, taking repeated measurements for the purpose of fixing the island's exact location, as well as gathering related data—for example, depth soundings along the shore and topographical information—necessary to draw accurate nautical charts and maps. The scientifics' work, Wilkes determined, was to be of secondary importance. Only after the ships spent the best part of the day, in pairs, moving from various locations off the coast in order to take the readings necessary for surveying would the scientifics be allowed to go ashore for just two hours to collect their own data and specimens. Needless to say, Wilkes's emphasis considerably irked the scientifics. Peale, for one, was unamused by the irony that a commander of a scientific expedition did not think "the resources of a land of equal importance with its hydrographic position."

Before the scientifics could be free to do their work, however, some sort of understanding had to be reached with the native inhabitants. At Clermont-Tonnerre, the expedition made its first contact with the Polynesians, as the native inhabitants of the many islands of the Pacific between New Zealand, Hawaii, and Easter Island are known. On their second day at the island, Wilkes and a landing party were greeted on the beach by 17 natives carrying spears and clubs; some 80 reinforcements lurked in the bush nearby. The expedition's interpreter, a Maori known as John Sac who had been taken from his New Zealand home by an American sea captain years earlier, translated their shouts as "Go to your own land; this belongs to us, and we do not want to have anything to do

Wilkes drew this diagram to show his officers how to conduct a "running survey" of an island, which involved taking measurements from a number of different points that constituted a framework of triangles over the object of measurement. Reynolds confessed that in surveying, the expedition "did as well as we could, but sometimes I was so perplexed that my brain was all in a whirl."

A colorfully tattooed native of the Tuamotu group, which the French explorer Louis-Antoine de Bougainville named the Dangerous Islands because of the numerous coral reefs found there. The islands were probably first settled by Polynesian seafarers from the Marquesas in the 15th century. By the time of Wilkes's visit pearl fishermen were landing regularly in the archipelago.

with you." The Polynesians brandished their weapons threateningly and prevented a landing.

Wilkes had earlier issued a general order declaring that the expedition's aims were "peace, good-will, and proper decorum to every class" and stipulating that "no act of hostility will be committed," but he had no intention "of letting them [Clermont-Tonnerre's inhabitants] see and feel that they had driven us off without landing." He ordered his men to fire upon the Polynesians with blank cartridges, then, when that tactic failed, with small pellets known as mustard-seed shot. After dignifiedly washing the blood from their wounded bodies, the Polynesians retreated into the forest.

The expedition's work at the other 16 of the Tuamotus it visited proceeded in similar fashion. Although there was no more bloodshed, misunderstandings between the newcomers and the natives continued. In his narratives, Wilkes characterized the natives of Serle Island, for example, as "arrant thieves . . . apparently without any idea that [stealing] was wrong." (Wilkes's accounts, and those of many other explorers, are filled with descriptions of thievery by native peoples. Many scholars believe that what those raised in a European or European-based culture interpreted as theft was the native peoples'—be they Polynesians, American Indians, or whatever—way of letting the newcomers know that they expected some sort of material compensation for use of, or passage through, their land.) His inept seamanship continued—off Serle one night, as Wilkes slept, the Vincennes crashed into the Porpoise; his response to the crisis was to run out on deck shouting, "My God! What is the matter? How is this? What shall we do?"—and the frustration of the scientifics mounted. While the navy men carried out their surveying and charting work, the scientifics fumed at remaining, as Peale put it, "all idle." Their discontent was especially pronounced at Honden, in the northeastern Tuamotus, a scientific paradise whose flora and fauna differed significantly from much of the rest of the archipelago. The island was uninhabited by humans but was home, in Reynolds's words, to "myriads of all varieties of the feathered tribes"; its many frigate birds, in particular, were so tame that "they actually suffered themselves to be plucked like fruit from the branches." Although Joseph Couthouy, the expedition's conchologist, observed that a complete exploration would have resulted in "a richer addition to our collections than a month passed at places which have been ransacked twenty times over," Wilkes allowed the scientifics only their standard two hours ashore. "What was a Scientific Corps sent for?" a disgusted Peale rhetorically asked in his correspondence.

Despite Wilkes's intransigence, the scientifics did succeed in doing much important work in the Tuamotus. It was here that Dana, the geologist, first observed and gathered the data that he cited to explain the evolutionary sequence that led from volcanic islands fringed with coral reefs to the disappearance of those islands and the creation of coral atolls surrounding a central lagoon. His theory had first been suggested by Charles Darwin, but Dana provided better evidence for its validity than the great English naturalist had been able to do. Horatio Hale, the expedition's ethnologist, would eventually produce an influential document, entitled "Chart of Oceanic Migrations," that illustrated the ancient westward movement of the Polynesians from their origin in Melanesia to the Tuamotus, Hawaii, and other archipelagos.

Spirits rose as the explorers neared the beautiful island of Tahiti, extolled by many European explorers as a kind of Eden. Even Wilkes, as the fleet approached, delighted in a rainbow "embracing a large part of the island, the colours of which were distinct and beautiful beyond description and made the scene almost look like a fairy land." At Matavai Bay, where the *Vincennes* dropped anchor on September 10, 1839, a stunning vista lay before them. Breadfruit, coconut, and orange groves lined the shores; rugged volcanic peaks towered in the distance.

Once ashore, the men of the expedition were even more

delighted, but for their self-proclaimed captain it was business as usual. One yeoman found the Tahitians to be "the most interesting people on the globe," and the sailors, after more than a year at sea, delighted in the friendly attentions of the Tahitian women, who are traditionally renowned for their beauty, although Wilkes found their figures "bad" and most of them "parrot-toed." An officer marveled that "never such a thing was seen or heard as a quarrel among them. . . . Every thing was harmony & playfullness & good humour." Wilkes, however, lamented their lack of initiative; the Tahitians, according to his narrative, were "generally to be found in their houses, in a circle, chatting, reading, and singing, or smoking, unless they be, as is often the case, asleep. They are seldom seen to be engaged in manual labour." The curmudgeonly commander was forced to admit that the Tahitian climate was "well adapted for the enjoyment of all the pleasures of life," but he did not wish his sailors to succumb to the island's charms. All hands were required to attend regular services at the bamboo church established and manned by Christian missionaries, and the port curfew (the time at which sailors were required to return to the ship) was changed from the customary 10:00 P.M. to sundown. Those comely young ladies who swam out to the ships in the predawn hours after singing and dancing on the pristine beaches were not, it almost goes without saying, permitted to board.

Under Wilkes's stern guidance, the expedition accomplished much during its stay at Tahiti, which lasted slightly more than a month. To the future gratitude of the captains of the 75 American whaling ships that called annually at the island, its 4 principal harbors were charted. In the interior, the scientifics measured the height of Orohena, one of Tahiti's highest peaks, and calculated the size and depth of Lake Waiherea. Wilkes concerned himself primarily with diplomacy, specifically with improving relations between the Tahitians and American government

(continued on page 65)

The Artistics

Lieutenant John Dale of the expedition painted this watercolor entitled View from Sugar Loaf Summit, Rio de Janeiro.

In the days before photography had been perfected as an art and a craft, the artist was an absolutely indispensable member of any self-respecting scientific expedition. No matter how skillfully they were used, words could only do so much to satisfy a public eager to know about the magnificent new worlds visited by daring explorers, and artifacts alone—say, an intricately carved war club from the Friendly Islands—did little to convey the sense of menace felt when it was brandished by a grimacing Fijian.

The scientifics could fill the holds of the ships of the U.S. Exploring Expedition (and later the galleries of museums) with specimens of coral, the preserved carcasses of frigate birds, assorted important artifacts and totems, even the skull of a cannibal, but only the "artistics"—primarily Alfred Agate and Joseph Drayton and to a lesser extent Titian Peale, but also those members of the expedition, including its captain, whose primary duty was not compiling a visual record of the voyage but who contributed their artistic efforts nonetheless—could show the view of Rio de Janeiro's harbor from the summit of Sugarloaf, the frigid majesty of ice in the Antarctic, the simmering, smoking inferno of Kilauea's caldera, and the delicate, intricate design of the innumerable creatures of the air, land, and sea they encountered.

Seemingly unperturbed by the presence of the Vincennes and the approach of one of its boats, seals lounge indolently on ice floes and cavort in the icy water of Disappointment Bay, as Wilkes named one of the inlets he encountered along the coast of Antarctica. At far left a shore party goes about its work; near the ship's stern sailors are swinging a huge chunk of ice aboard, to be used as a source of fresh water. This painting was done by Wilkes himself.

The infernal Kilauea, Night Scene *was done in oil by Peale, the expedition's naturalist, probably from his on-the-spot sketches and notes many years after the expedition was completed.*

Agate painted this portrait of King Kamehameha III of Hawaii in a resplendent military-style uniform. By 1840, most Hawaiians wore a combination of traditional and European-style clothing, with royalty almost always dressing in European garb.

Drayton's field drawing of Bodianus loxozonus (*above*), a type of wrasse, or elongated, spiny-finned fish, taken off Sertes Island in the Tuamotus, and of a specimen of Corris flavovitta (*below*) that was captured by native Hawaiian fishermen in their nets. Agate and Drayton, the expedition's two artists, were officially members of the scientific team; their skill at faithful reproduction was essential to the later accurate classification and analysis by the scientifics and other scientists of the many species of flora and fauna encountered on the expedition.

Peale drew this field sketch of a Laysan albatross on Wake Island on May 26, 1841. Such sketches formed the basis for the ornate full-color plates that, in this particular case, illustrated the expedition's official volume on its bird and mammal collections.

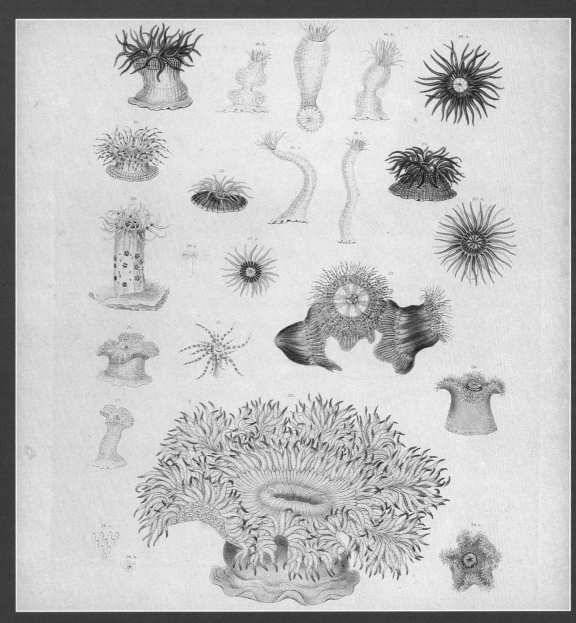

Drayton's painting of a sea anemone (bottom, at center) and similar organisms illustrated the atlas to the expedition's volume Zoophytes. The most important work of the report on zoophytes was James Dwight Dana's ground-breaking work on corals, which two of the foremost European authorities on the subject called "one of the most valuable contributions which America has yet made to Natural History."

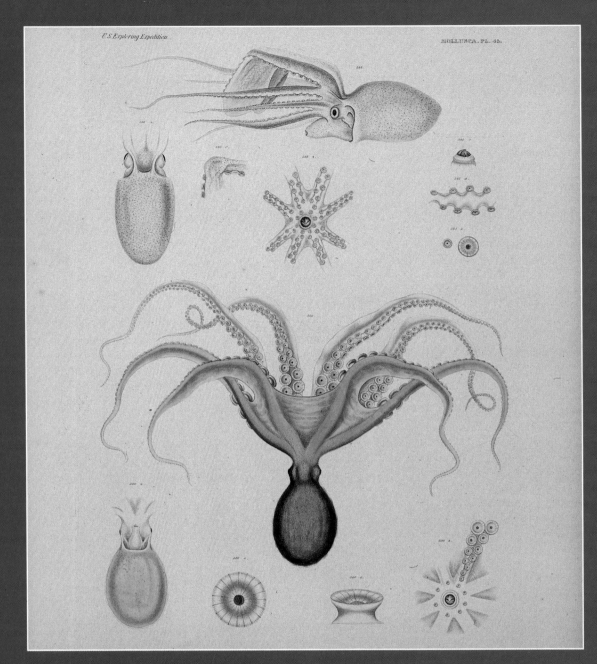

Because cephalopod specimens
were so difficult to preserve in
the field and in storage, Drayton's
portrayals of the two octopi seen here
were particularly important to the
scientific community.

A *rural road in Tahiti, from Wilkes's narratives. The first European explorers to visit Tahiti—the Englishmen Samuel Wallis and Cook and the Frenchman Bougainville— believed they had found a kind of Eden. They were united in their delight over the beautiful climate and landscape and the handsomeness, innocence, and liberated sexual practices of the Tahitians. Cook's men considered themselves "imparadised" while they were there.*

(continued from page 56)

officials, which had grown strained. Diplomacy would not seem to have been a pursuit for which he was ideally suited, and the chief result of his efforts was a feud between himself and Samuel Blackler, the U.S. consul. Wilkes tried, unsuccessfully, to have Blackler removed from office, for the alleged offenses of bringing liquor onto the island in contravention of local law and imposing arbitrary and cruel punishments upon American seamen.

The contrast between the paradise that was Tahiti and nearby islands visited by the *Vincennes* and the *Porpoise* and the hell that was service under Wilkes was apparently too much for some sailors, and several deserted before the fleet set sail. Motivated by a reward of $150 offered by Wilkes, the Tahitians captured the deserters, who were returned bound by their hands and feet to long poles, which their captors carried over their shoulders. Each deserter was ordered to pay his captor the reward Wilkes had promised and then received 36 lashes.

Wilkes (seen here), wrote Dana, "was a man without conciliation, inclined to be arbitrary in minor matters as well as those that were important, and often at variance with some of his officers."
He has remained the subject of historical controversy to the present day: Was he simply a self-aggrandizing tyrant, or were his excesses and failings redeemed by his dedication to important and worthy goals?

Hundreds of canoes followed the *Peacock* and *Flying Fish*, the last two ships to depart, as they stood to sea in early October. Not a "single soul," one seaman wrote, left "this simple & kind hearted people" without regret, but Wilkes was eager to reach Sydney, Australia, in time to make another assault on Antarctica during the polar summer. Accordingly, the fleet was split up, as it had been in the Tuamotus, so as to facilitate the maximum amount of exploration in the minimum amount of time. The most significant work was done in the Navigator Islands, which are more popularly referred to as Samoa. During the month they spent there, the expedition's officers conscientiously made astronomical, magnetic, and meteorological observations, kept a complete record of the tides, and surveyed the coasts of all seven islands. Occasionally, these duties entailed unexpected discomforts. On Upolu, for example, Reynolds and several others tramped 80 miles to survey a harbor. The trek "across mountains where the paths were steep, narrow and rough, raining most of the time, was rather trying to us, who have done but little in the pedestrian way save walking on smooth planks for more than a year," he wrote, although he took some consolation in the "superb and glorious scenery of the island and the gentle nature of the people."

Meanwhile, Peale romped about the same isle, climbing an extinct volcano, collecting a variety of specimens of birds, and measuring everything from waterfalls to banyan trees; and Wilkes decided to introduce the natives to American justice. Tuvai, a Samoan man, had allegedly earlier murdered a sailor from an American sailing ship. Convinced that such misdeeds could not be allowed to go unpunished, particularly in light of the increased American commerce in the region that the expedition's work was to encourage, Wilkes had his officers capture the miscreant. He then sat as judge and jury, pronounced the unfortunate Tuvai guilty, and sentenced him to exile in some remote place "where he would never again have an opportunity [for] killing a white man," according to the narratives. The convicted murderer traveled with the fleet when it left Samoa and was then presented by Wilkes as a gift to a native chief on Wallis Island.

Tuvai's feelings about all this were not recorded, but Wilkes's disdainful attitude toward the native peoples of the Pacific constituted yet another difference between himself and those under his command, most of whom had come to harbor considerable respect for the new ways of life they had encountered. Many, like Reynolds, disliked the supposed "civilizing influences" that the Europeans and Americans were bringing to the region, of which the expedition was itself a manifestation and Wilkes an unquestioning champion. "I could not help thinking," he wrote, "how much better it would be to let [the natives] go their own old way, but No! No! We must have all the world like us, if we can." By this point, dislike for their commander had united navy man and scientific. An expedition physician referred to him as the "most contemptible of petty tyrants," and according to Reynolds "he had become in the eyes of the whole Squadron a false and malignant villain—no milder term will do."

While in Samoa, the explorers observed a number of native dances. Many members of the expedition came to lament the effect that western influences were having on the traditional way of life in the Pacific, particularly, according to Reynolds, the "gross, absurd tissue of nonsense, ignorance, and fanaticism" spread there by American missionaries.

No Mistake About It

The *Vincennes* and the *Peacock* reached Sydney after nightfall on November 29, followed the next day by the *Porpoise* and the *Flying Fish*. Undaunted by his navigational mishaps, Wilkes declined to hire a local pilot to guide him through the tricky harbor—he did, however, have on board a former Sydney trader—and brought the *Vincennes* in under cover of darkness, the *Peacock* cautiously following. The stunt earned him plaudits from the local press, which sang the praises of Yankee "nautical skill and daring." The explorers were also pleased, Wilkes wrote, glad to be "once more in a civilized country, and one where their own language was spoken." Then a city of 24,000, Sydney, the first British settlement in Australia, had been founded in 1787 as a penal colony; in the years since, Britain had shipped more than 100,000 convicts—men, women, and children—halfway around the world to Australia's shores, "the largest forced exile of citizens at the behest of a European government in pre-modern history," according to historian Robert Hughes.

Sydney society reflected the city's origins, as the members of the expedition discovered once they began going about ashore. Reynolds wrote that "the richest people here were convicts. . . . One man has built himself a house on the very spot where stood the gallows, to which gallows he had been taken three times with the Rope around his neck!" Although the expedition's members received and

Lieutenant William L. Hudson, portrayed here by Agate, captained the Peacock *and served as Wilkes's second-in-command. When Wilkes promoted himself to captain, he thoughtfully promoted his friend Hudson as well.*

accepted many invitations to some of Sydney's finest homes (a good number of them owned by former convicts), many also enjoyed spending time east of George Street, "the Broadway of Sydney," a section of town filled, according to the puritanical Wilkes, with "grog-shops and brothels." The commander deplored the widespread public drunkenness he witnessed—a vice for which Australia was notorious—and was appalled that "even persons of the fairer sex (if they may be so called)" staggered along the streets, brawled in the taverns, and were carted off to jail. Members of his crew, however, made themselves right at home in such taverns as the Punch-Bowl, the Ship, and the Jolly Sailors. While the ships were overhauled and supplies were loaded, the scientifics prepared their Pacific collections for shipment home and journeyed into the bush. In his narratives, Wilkes described the Australian countryside as desolate and arid, but the scientifics found it fascinating. During one 3-mile hike, for example, William Brackenridge and William Rich, the expedition's botanists, collected 150 specimens. The continent's animal life was equally abundant and intriguing; having broken off from Antarctica some 40 million years ago, Australia had developed in evolutionary isolation, and there were numerous species to be examined there—the kangaroo, the spiny anteater, the duck-billed platypus, and the koala bear, to name just 4—that lived nowhere else in the world.

Finally, Australia provided rich subject matter for ethnological study in the aborigines, as the members of the

This engraving of Australian aborigines performing one of their traditional dances graced the pages of Wilkes's narratives. The ritual nocturnal ceremonies at which such dances and songs were performed are known as corroborees.

hundreds of nomadic tribes that had once been the continent's sole human inhabitants were collectively known. Brutalized and deracinated by the white conquerors of the continent, the aborigines were suspended between a new, essentially European culture that they wanted no part of and a traditional way of life that had been ineradicably altered. Alcohol, introduced to them by the British, had had a devastating effect; Wilkes cold-bloodedly predicted that the "ravages of intoxication and disease, combined with their occasional warfare" would mean their imminent extinction. While traveling in the interior, the scientifics encountered several aboriginal groups and even had the privilege of viewing some tribal ceremonies.

For once, the scientifics would have ample time for their explorations, for Wilkes decided that they would remain behind while the remainder of the expedition again attempted to reach Antarctica. (He did, however, dismiss their request for a ship to be used to explore the many nearby islands.) While the fleet was again braving the polar ice, the scientifics were to employ themselves "as may be most conducive to the interests of the Expedition," taking care to make "all possible collections" and maintain a "minute journal." Upon rejoining the expedition on March 1, 1840, at New Zealand's Bay of Islands, they were to submit a full written report of their activities. Over the next three months the scientifics would engage in a variety of endeavors in a number of different locations, adding a great number of specimens to their collections. The artists completed a large number of drawings and paintings, and many maps and charts were drawn. Dana again did significant work, this time on the geological history of Australia. Hale also distinguished himself: Although his theory that the aborigines all spoke dialects of a single language rather than separate tongues has since been discounted, he did collect the single most important artifact that the scientifics gathered from Australia—an

Australian aborigines—the black-skinned native inhabitants of the continent—make their way through the forest in this illustration from Wilkes's narratives. Disease, loss of their traditional lands, and a systematic campaign of extermination had drastically reduced the aboriginal population in the little more than 50 years between the beginning of European settlement in 1788 and the arrival of the Exploring Expedition.

Ship surgeon Charles Guillou drew this pencil sketch of the Peacock *trapped in the ice during its second Antarctic voyage. According to Reynolds, Guillou "was the only one, who had exhibited visible signs of perturbation [while the ship was in danger]—poor man, every one noticed his nervous anxiety—he was in every body's way & asking questions which had better not been breathed."*

elaborately engraved aboriginal rug, made from opossum and kangaroo skins and worn as protection against the cold or as a burial wrap. There are only seven such rugs in existence today.

Meanwhile, the squadron left Sydney, headed south, on December 26. Wilkes had named Macquarie Island, some 2,100 miles southeast of Sydney, as a rendezvous point in order to ensure that the fleet stayed together, for reasons of safety, but after the *Flying Fish* became disabled and Wilkes callously sailed away aboard the *Vincennes* (an act that his men attributed to his desire to claim all the glory of discovering Antarctica for himself), each ship was on its own. The *Vincennes* and the *Porpoise* sailed past Macquarie without stopping; the *Peacock* halted, but on the opposite side of the island from the crippled *Flying Fish*, and the battered schooner then continued southward without any knowledge of the whereabouts of the remainder of the fleet. In addition to the damage sustained in the New Year's Day blow, its decks leaked so badly that it was necessary, according to Wilkes's narratives, "to keep the pumps going almost constantly." Injury and illness claimed several members of its crew, which was already undermanned because of desertions, and during one particularly brutal storm the lookouts were forced to lash themselves to the foremast so as not to be swept overboard into the raging sea. On February 5, the demoralized crew issued Lieutenant Robert Pinkney, the commander, an ultimatum. It read, in part: "We are in a most deplorable condition: the bed clothes are all wet; we have no place to lie down in; we have not had a stitch of dry clothing for seven days . . . and we . . . can hold out no longer; we hope you will take it into consideration, and relieve us from what must terminate in our death." Pinkney's only option, the crew stated, was to order the ship to head for milder latitudes. The lieutenant, who was quite ill himself, agreed to do so, and the *Flying Fish* reached the Bay of Islands on March 9.

The other ships fared better. Less than three weeks out from Sydney, the men of the *Peacock* began seeing familiar sights—penguins, whales, and gargantuan icebergs, eerie in their silent majesty and power. "We all came on deck . . . and we all gazed, till our very vision ached, on the dazzling ice that we were passing by," an officer recorded. At about 10 o'clock on the morning of January 16, 1840, as the *Peacock* drifted parallel to a seemingly impenetrable barrier of ice hundreds of feet tall, Reynolds and a sailor named Henry Eld climbed into the rigging to take advantage of the unusually clear weather to take some sightings. In the distance, they saw "conical forms" that suggested mountains. One of them scrambled down for a spyglass, the use of which caused the mountainous terrain of that portion of Antarctica now known as George V Coast to "burst upon [them] with the utmost vividness," according to Reynolds. Eld estimated the mountains to be 2,000 feet high; their height alone, he wrote, was "enough to establish [Antarctica's] identity, for no berg or Ice Island Ever seen was one quarter its Altitude." Yet Captain Hudson remained unmoved by their report and refused to go aloft to make a confirmation, and officer of the deck Thomas Budd failed to record it in the log.

Two days afterward, the entire crew of the *Peacock* had a clear glimpse of the Antarctic region now known as Mawson's Peninsula. Several days later, the *Peacock* obtained further evidence that Antarctica was a continent, in the form of rock fragments culled from the ocean and pebbles taken from a penguin's craw. With such incontrovertible proof, the matter of Reynolds's and Eld's overlooked first sighting faded into the background, particularly after the ship, sailing close in an attempt to prove Hudson's theory that the ice barrier rested on solid ground, became trapped among the towering bergs early on the morning of January 24. A succession of tremendous crashes brought breakfasting officers to the deck, where it was discovered that the ship's rudder had been torn away. The *Peacock* could now no longer be steered, and icebergs played glacial pinball with the man-of-war as it drifted helplessly toward the barrier. As the ship's carpenters worked frantically to fashion a new rudder, several sailors took to the frigid waters in small boats and tried to fasten ice anchors to icebergs in the hope of slowing the *Peacock*'s progress, but the anchors would not hold. The crisis elicited a variety of responses: One officer remembered his family and despaired that "almost certain death stared us in the face," while Eld, strangely detached, noted in his journal the "grandeur and beauty of this stupendous Mountain of Ice." Convinced that "a few moments would send us to the bottom," Reynolds considered his options and decided that "any struggle for life would be in vain: to reach a piece of Ice would only be to linger in agony and suffer a more horrible death, and I settled in my mind with startling quickness that it would be best to go down with the Ship."

Captain Hudson, however, was focused on saving the ship and with a number of stratagems and some good luck succeeded in turning it around so that when it struck the ice barrier, it did so stern first. Prepared by Hudson's orders, the *Peacock*'s crew quickly made sail as the ship recoiled from the concussion, and the vessel stood out from the barrier in just enough time to avoid a collapsing ice ledge that would have "crushed [it] to atoms," according to Wilkes's narratives. Colliding with icebergs "as if she would knock herself to pieces," as Reynolds put it, the *Peacock* floundered toward open water. A makeshift rudder was rigged the next morning, and the ship limped back to Sydney, which it reached on February 21 after a "long, stormy, and anxious voyage."

That same day, Wilkes terminated the *Vincennes*'s polar voyage and directed his ship toward Sydney. A lookout on his ship, James Alden, had spotted land on the morning of January 19, but Wilkes, like Hudson, dismissed the report and failed to record it. It was not until 9 days later, when the flagship reached Piner Bay on the Adelie Coast,

This map done by Wilkes, entitled "Chart of the Antarctic Continent Shewing the Icy Barrier Attached to It," documented Antarctica's existence as a continent for the first time. He named many of the coastline's geographic features after his ships and crew—Peacocks Bay, Cape Hudson, Reynold's Peak, Eld's Peak, etc.

with its 3,600-foot mountains, that Wilkes admitted "there is no mistake about it"—the *Vincennes* had reached Antarctica. His subsequent reconnaissance and charting of 1,500 miles of the coastline proved beyond a doubt the continent's existence, but to his consternation, when the *Vincennes* returned to Sydney on March 11, he learned that the celebrated French explorer of the Pacific, Jules-Sébastien-César Dumont d'Urville, whose two-ship fleet (one of them the famous *Astrolabe*) the *Porpoise* had encountered near the ice barrier on January 30, was claiming that he had sighted the land mass of Antarctica on January 20. The Americans' claim to priority of discovery was thus threatened, as the first sightings that they could verify by recordings in their ships' logs had not occurred until after Dumont d'Urville's. Suddenly, Wilkes had reason to credit Alden's sighting, as did Hudson with Reynolds and Eld's claims, and the commander later doctored his flagship's log and tailored his narratives accordingly. The ensuing controversy over first sighting, which raged for years, detracted from the incontrovertible achievements of the South Seas Exploring Expedition in proving Antarctica's existence as a continent, particularly Wilkes's charting of so much of the coastline. His probity was questioned, even in his own country, and the famed British polar explorer James Clark Ross, who reached Antarctica later in 1840, went so far as to claim that Wilkes never got there at all.

This engraving was done from Wilkes's own drawing of his flagship anchored near an ice island on the second Antarctic voyage, during which he ignored the warning of the ship's doctors that his men were in grave danger because of exposure. "I came to the conclusion, at whatever hazard to ship and crew, that it was my duty to proceed," he wrote later. The dog, a pet Wilkes obtained while in Australia, was named Sydney.

A Black Train of Consequences

After a couple of weeks spent basking in Australian admiration for his polar exploits, Wilkes set sail in the *Vincennes* for New Zealand on March 30, 1840. (The *Flying Fish* and the *Porpoise* had gone directly to the Bay of Islands; the *Peacock*, which remained behind in Sydney to finish receiving badly needed repairs, headed directly for the island group of Tonga, the expedition's next destination.) There, he was reunited with the scientifics, who were impatient and bored, having, according to Peale, "gathered all the plants, shot all the Birds, caught all the fish, and got heartily sick of the Natives, in spite of their tatooing and carving."

The squadron took a somewhat roundabout route to Tonga, enabling it to determine the position of some nearby islands and the nonexistence of others purported to lie in the region. On April 24, after 18 days at sea, the *Vincennes* called at Tongatapu and Eooa, the southernmost of the Friendly Islands, as Cook had dubbed the group today more commonly referred to as Tonga. On May 4 the reunited fleet—the *Peacock* had arrived on May 1—headed west again for Fiji (commonly rendered Feejee or Feegee in Wilkes's day), an archipelago comprising 800 islands, only about 100 of them inhabited. At first sight, Fiji appeared to be another paradise. Reynolds described Ovalau, then the island most favored by European settlers and sailors, as "high and clothed in the most luxuriant

The Fijian chief Tanoa, with whom Wilkes concluded a trade agreement, was, according to the lieutenant, "about sixty-five years old, tall, slender, and rather bent by age, . . . His countenance was indicative of intelligence and shrewdness."

In long huts on the islands of Fiji—such as this one drawn by Agate—bêche-de-mer was dried after having been boiled. The dried sea cucumbers were then transported for sale in China.

verdure, with many bold points of rock and immense forests; and here and there shining waterfalls glanced amid the foliage." But Fiji's beauty belied its unsettling reputation as the "Cannibal Islands," and several officers drew up their wills during the rainy passage from Tongatapu. Wilkes thought the islands so breathtaking that he admitted he could barely bring himself to believe that "they were the abode of a savage, ferocious, and treacherous race of cannibals."

Although Fiji was well known to ship captains, who ventured there for sandalwood, turtle shells, and bêche-de-mer (also known as trepang, sea cucumbers, and sea slugs; when boiled and dried, they were highly prized by the Chinese as a delicacy and aphrodisiac), it had never been accurately charted. Surrounded by dangerous coral reefs and shoals, the islands appeared on available maps ominously embellished with the names of ships wrecked upon their shores, and their inhabitants had made a tradition of scavenging from scuttled vessels, believing that a castaway ship was a gift from the gods. Fiji's reputation was such that Wilkes claimed "that he expected to lose two of his vessels" there, although Reynolds dismissed this utterance "as all fudge and uttered for effect."

In order to carry out his ambitious plan for charting Fiji, Wilkes found it necessary to divide his force. Only the *Flying Fish*, of his primary vessels, was small enough to be suited for the work; it was dispatched to map the islands south and east of Viti Levu, the largest island. The *Porpoise* was sent to the easternmost islands, while the responsibility for charting the rest of the islands fell to small teams manning the launches and cutters from the remaining two ships. These were sent out for several weeks at a time with the admonition to "avoid landing any where on the main land or islands, unless the latter should be uninhabited."

All told, the surveying took three months; the work was "excruciating and unceasing," according to one weary sailor. The boats used were 28 or 32 feet long and carried at least 5 sailors, who were required to work, eat, and sleep on board, with, according to Reynolds, "no more room for exercise than a chicken in a shell." The nights were chilly and damp, leading Reynolds to complain that every morning his "bones were as sore as if I had been well beaten with a bunch of clubs and then shoved under a pump." Often, the crews survived on short rations, and in defiance of Wilkes's orders they went ashore to trade for pigs and yams with the natives, who at other times were less helpful. Enamored of the bright colors of the station flags that the surveyors used to mark and measure the angles between landmarks, the Fijians pilfered them.

The officers and crew of the *Flying Fish*, meanwhile, had problems of their own—most notably, the frequent presence of Wilkes, who often insisted on accompanying

While some members of the Exploring Expedition watch from outside a chief's hut, Fijians perform the meke wau, *or club dance. The engraving was based on a drawing by expedition artist Joseph Drayton. Such meke were performances of sung poetry accompanied by a dance depicting mythical and historical battles and were presented as gestures of friendship from one sovereign nation to another.*

Along with 2 others collected by the expedition, this carved wooden female figure, about 18 inches in height, is the earliest known Fijian figure currently in museum collections. The 1,200 Fijian artifacts obtained by the expedition, most of which are housed in the Smithsonian Institution, constitute 1 of the 3 most important such collections in the world.

them. The obstinate captain knew next to nothing about the schooner's fore-and-aft rigs and less about the perilous local reefs and currents, but he consistently overrode the advice of a local pilot nonetheless and finally ran the ship aground on Goat Island. Lieutenant Sinclair wrote, "I never, in my life, have seen a man handle a vessel as Capt. Wilkes does."

Wilkes fared better with Tanoa, the wizened chief from Ambau, an island west of Ovalau, whose approval he wished to obtain for an agreement guaranteeing protection to American ships and sailors while in Fiji. During a state visit aboard the *Vincennes* in May, Tanoa was honored with a cannon salute, presents (including accordions and whales' teeth), and a feast of ricebread and molasses. "Old Snuff," as the chief was known to the whites because he constantly looked as if he were about to sneeze, and his sizable retinue "whooped their surprise and pleasure aloud," reported Reynolds, who, to his dismay, became one of the chief's great favorites. (In his youth, the chief had been a fearsome warrior, reputed to have eaten many of his slain enemies, and Reynolds worried that Tanoa might indulge his palate at his expense.) The feasting had its desired effect, however, and Tanoa signed the agreement.

The captain's other dealings with the Fijians ended less satisfactorily. At Wilkes's orders, Hudson had taken into custody Vendovi, a local chief responsible for the killing of 10 American sailors from the trading ship *Charles Doggett* some 7 years earlier. After a summary trial, Hudson pronounced Vendovi guilty and sentenced him to exile in the United States, where he would learn that "to kill a white person was the very worst thing a Feegee could do," as Reynolds put it. But the lesson thus supposedly imparted was lost on its intended recipients, as Hudson quickly learned when a Fijian proclaimed that he had also always wanted to see America and that now he supposed the best way to do so was to kill an American.

Vendovi's capture, which Hudson had accomplished by tricking the Fijian's family and friends and then taking them hostage, led to considerable tension between the Fijians and their American visitors. Fearing retaliation, Wilkes doubled the guard at the encampment and observatory he had established on Ovalau near the port of Levuka. The explorers' unrest increased when one member of a friendly group of natives who visited the *Vincennes* in early July was discovered to be eating the flesh from a human head, nonchalantly "gnawing away," according to Reynolds, "on the bloody muscles of the Eye with evident relish and calling out good, good." The crew could see cooked human legs garnished with baked yams on a bed of plantain leaves in the canoe pulled up alongside the flagship. "The smell the smell. I never shall forget it. It inough to make a mans blood run cold to think of sutch," one sailor wrote, his revulsion clearly expressed despite his imperfect spelling and usage. "Every one on the ship was affected with a nervous & terrible feeling of mingled horror & disgust," Reynolds wrote, although the scientifics, in the spirit of scholarly inquiry, overcame their repugnance long enough to purchase the head as a specimen for their collections.

On July 11, a surveying party working off Vanua Levu, an island 38 miles northeast of Viti Levu, inadvertently allowed the cutter from the *Vincennes* to wash ashore. The boat was laden with more than $1,000 worth of trade goods, provisions, and scientific instruments, which the island's inhabitants, as was their longtime custom, claimed as their own. They did not, however, harm any of the members of the expedition. When he learned of the incident, Wilkes became incensed and set sail in the *Flying Fish* for Vanua Levu. The Fijians were persuaded to return the boat (with only a few items missing), but the captain remained unsatisfied: At his orders, on July 14 the village of Tye was burned to the ground.

Ten days after the assault on Tye, members of a survey

Agate's portrait of Lieutenant William Underwood, whose death on Malolo led to a U.S. attack on the island. Underwood's friend William May wrote that the lieutenant "had not his superior, if equal, in the Navy—he was very talented, spoke fluently French, Spanish & Italian, was a profound mathematician & surveyor."

party went ashore on the island of Malolo, on the western periphery of Fiji, to secure some food. Under the command of Lieutenant William Underwood and Midshipman Wilkes Henry, who was Wilkes's nephew, the party took the usual precaution of securing a hostage while they bargained for a pig and some yams, but when the hostage escaped, an ambush was sprung. Reynolds, who was on the scene, wrote that the two officers, realizing that their own escape was impossible, "directed the men to save themselves and commenced the goodly work of avenging their own sad fate." Underwood was last seen pulling a spear from his shoulder with both hands and ordering his men to the boats. "There was such a crowd and confusion, and the natives swarmed so thick, that those in the boats could not see what was going on until the shots that were fired warned them that there was bloody work," Reynolds wrote, and Underwood and Henry were both clubbed to death.

The slain officers "were the two," Reynolds wrote, "above all others, who had the most enviable reputation in the Squadron." Upon hearing the news, Wilkes, who was five miles away from Malolo in the *Flying Fish*, retreated to the cockpit and wept. The incident, he confided in a letter to his wife, had left him temporarily unfit for duty. One may wonder, however, if the captain was shedding crocodile tears for Underwood, whom he had repeatedly accused of masterminding a conspiracy to undermine his leadership and whose death, he revealed privately to his confidants, was caused by his overconfidence. On the afternoon of their death, Wilkes had Underwood and Henry buried "deep in pure white sand" on a distant island far removed from the "condor-eyed" cannibals of Malolo.

The next day, the United States South Seas Exploring Expedition invaded Malolo. Wilkes's assault on the town of Arro on the north side of the island, to be launched from the *Flying Fish*, bogged down when he ran the ship aground on a shoal, but the main attack force on the south shore fulfilled the captain's orders to "destroy every thing save women & children." While several landing parties were put ashore, rockets launched from the cutters set the Fijians' palisades ablaze. An estimated 87 Fijians were killed in the attack, and several villages and entire crops of sugarcane, yams, and taro were destroyed in a spectacular blaze one officer described as "grand, & beautiful and at the same time horrible." Wilkes declined to make peace with the Fijians until they sued for it in their traditional fashion—by crawling on their hands and knees to a parley with the victors and begging for mercy.

The bloodletting appeased Wilkes. "I feel conscious I have done my duty," he wrote his wife, "inflicted severe punishment tempered with mercy and fully avenged the death of Poor Wilkes & Lt. Underwood." On August 11, to the relief of virtually every member of the expedition, the fleet set sail for the Sandwich Islands, as Cook had named what is known today as Hawaii. (The *Vincennes* and the *Peacock* proceeded directly there while the other two ships tended to some unfinished business, including a survey of the great coral reef along Vanua Levu's northern coastline, which the *Flying Fish* conducted, and the rescue of shipwrecked American whalers from the island of Vatoa, which the *Porpoise* carried out.) "We hated the looks of the people, and we were tired with the harassing work," Reynolds wrote. For once, captain and subordinate agreed. Despite the expedition's many successes in Fiji— the scientifics had gathered literally hundreds of plant, coral, and crustacean specimens and more than a thousand artifacts, the surveyors had done ground- and backbreaking work, and Dana continued his innovative theorizing—"on taking our final departure from these islands, all of us felt great pleasure," Wilkes recalled in his narratives. Reynolds added an emphatic amen: "I trust never to see them again."

Malolo burns in retaliation for the death of Underwood and Wilkes Henry, the only son of Wilkes's sister Eliza. Lieutenant George Emmons drew this sketch in his journal of the expedition.

More Monster
than Man

Wilkes intended Hawaii to be little more than a brief stop for reprovisioning and rest. The archipelago had already been thoroughly charted, and he was eager for the expedition to move on to Oregon, where important geopolitical work awaited it. But the full squadron was not anchored in the harbor at Honolulu, a city on the southeast coast of the island of Oahu, until October 8, 1840, too late in the season to begin work at Oregon, where the winter months were notoriously cold, rainy, and dreary.

The climate in Hawaii was much more appealing, but the delay meant that the expedition would have to be extended for at least another year, a prospect that dismayed most of the enlisted men. For the majority, their three-year term of duty expired on November 1, and few were eager to reenlist, for relations between Wilkes and his crew had continued to be poor. In Australia, before and after the Antarctic voyage, he had suspended and reprimanded medical personnel for what he regarded as impertinent comments in their letters, quarreled with officers and the scientifics, fulminated constantly against cabals, and driven many men to desertion. On the long, monotonous northeast passage to Hawaii, the temporary solidarity created by the Malolo tragedy had broken down. Wilkes again began arbitrarily transferring officers between ships, and he argued with Hudson, one of his few friends on the expedition, whom he blamed for losing the survey notes

Agate's sketch of a tattooed Pacific Islands native. William H. Goetzmann believes that for various reasons, cultural relativism—the attempt to understand a foreign culture on its own terms rather than those of the observer—"came more naturally as a concept to South Seas adventurers than to any other group long before anthropologists formalized the term."

pertaining to Samoa. The crew's unrest was aggravated by short rations; Reynolds wrote that aboard the Peacock "nothing but water and bread crumbs for breakfast was all we had for more than once, and supper was not spoken of, by mutual consent." The result, in Hawaii, was a severely demoralized crew that at last had the opportunity to remedy its discontent.

Wilkes had no intention of letting the expedition be undermined so close to completion. He and his officers attempted to appeal to the patriotism of their sailors; when that failed, they offered financial inducements, in the form of reenlistment bonuses, and extra shore leave. When this did not work, Wilkes, in contravention of naval regulations, informed those who did not wish to re-up that they would be abandoned in Hawaii to arrange their own transportation home. After drinking up a goodly portion of their pay in Honolulu's grog shops, most of the crews of the ships other than the Vincennes decided to sign on for the duration, but 48 of those who had to serve directly under Wilkes aboard the flagship decided to remain in Hawaii. The captain hired on 50 Hawaiians to replace them and persuaded 3 sailors to return to service by clapping them in irons and publicly flogging them. The whipping incident somehow did not make it into Wilkes's five volumes of expedition narratives, and despite the ample evidence that he was driving his men too hard, the captain did not change his style: While in Hawaii, he arrested one officer and a physician for impudence and disrespect and later had them tried in a court-martial.

Despite the enforced layover, Wilkes did not mean for the expedition to become idle. "I was averse to passing our time in comparative inactivity," he related in the narratives, and, almost alone among the myriad travelers who have visited Oahu, he was not enchanted by its physical beauty. He had expected "a perfect garden" but found himself confronted instead with a land "by no means inviting" that he described as rocky, barren, and almost desertlike. Undistracted by Oahu's natural charms, he therefore busied himself with establishing several scientific observatories, diplomatic visits to the governor and King Kamehameha III, and leading an expedition to the summit of Mauna Loa, a 14,000-foot active volcano on the island of Hawaii. The climb to the summit, which began in mid-December, took nine days to complete. Wilkes's party of 19 was accompanied by 200 native porters, bearing every variety of provisions and equipment, as well as their wives and children, a bull, and 40 hogs. This unlikely procession stretched out for more than two miles; it resembled, wrote Wilkes, a "May-day morning in New York." Despite suffering from snow blindness and altitude sickness, Wilkes and his men spent several weeks in their observatory and encampment near the summit, taking measurements and atmospheric readings and examining "the craters and late eruptions." After their descent, Wilkes visited the nearby volcano of Kilauea, where another expedition team, in-

Joseph Drayton drew this view of the smoldering summit crater of the volcano of Kilauea, on the island of Hawaii, with the aid of a camera lucida, a 19th-century optical instrument and forerunner of the modern camera that projected an image of an object onto a plane surface so that its outline could be traced.

Bearing tridents edged with shark teeth and protected by cocoa-fiber vests, warriors on Drummond Island in the Kingsmill group advance. The drawing is by Agate. On Drummond Island, the disappearance of a member of the crew of the Peacock *triggered the Exploring Expedition's second attack.*

cluding Dana, was exploring. Wilkes speculated that the entire city of New York would fit within the massive crater, but he was nonetheless somewhat disappointed at the lack of pyrotechnics: "I saw nothing before us but a huge pit, black, ill-looking, and totally different from what I had expected. There were no jets of fire, no eruptions of heated stones, no cones, nothing but a depression."

Although the U.S. consul in Hawaii expressed his admiration of Wilkes's "iron-hearted energy and perseverance" in a letter to the secretary of state, the men of the expedition were less impressed. While the scientifics were fanning out over the interiors of Kauai, Oahu, and Hawaii in search of specimens, Wilkes, as he had vowed to do, sent Hudson in the *Peacock*, Cadwalader Ringgold in the *Porpoise*, and R. F. Pinkney in the *Flying Fish* back to resurvey Samoa. While there, Hudson attempted, in fulfillment of Wilkes's orders, to "obtain ample justice for the late murder of an American seaman on that island," but he was unable to capture the killer. Frustrated, he and his men set fire to several villages instead. Reynolds, for one, was unhappy with a policy that required the expedition "to take life, to pay for life," particularly after the explorers torched the village of Utiroa on Drummond Island in the Kingsmill group (today the island is known as Tabiteuea and its group as the Gilbert Islands) in retaliation for the murder of a *Peacock* seaman. "Our path through the Pacific is to be marked in blood," Reynolds lamented.

After his return to Honolulu, Wilkes occupied himself with further diplomatic tasks—a dinner hosted by several Oahu chiefs at which they served dog, disguised as pork (the head of a swine was sewn onto the mongrel's body), was a particular highlight—and readying the fleet for its spring departure. During this time, at Kamehameha's request, Wilkes and the men of the *Vincennes* successfully charted Pearl Harbor, which the captain believed would someday be "the best and most capacious harbor in the

Pacific," but upon the arrival of the *Porpoise* in Honolulu on March 23, Wilkes insisted on overseeing its repair himself. As he bellowed instructions in front of a large crowd of onlookers in Honolulu harbor, the 224-ton brig was raised into the air so that carpenters could recopper its hull, only to topple ignominiously onto the wharf because of an oversight on Wilkes's part. "I could have crawled into the bunghold of the smallest sized water breaker," one mortified officer wrote. To the expedition's continued embarrassment, it took 11 days to raise the *Porpoise*; once it was righted, Wilkes ordered it to make sail, with the *Vincennes*, for Oregon, where the 2 ships were scheduled to rendezvous on May 1 with the *Peacock* and the *Flying Fish*, then still in the South Pacific.

At the time, the Oregon Country comprised all or part of present-day Oregon, Washington, Idaho, and British Columbia and was claimed by both Britain and the United States. The most important waterway in the region was the Columbia River, which enters the Pacific Ocean after flowing west for several hundred miles along what is today the border between the states of Washington and Oregon. The Exploring Expedition's mission was to chart and survey the Columbia, its tributaries, and surrounding regions so as to provide the U.S. government with a more detailed and accurate idea of the Oregon Country's geography, resources, and potential for settlement.

The *Vincennes* and the *Porpoise* reached the mouth of the Columbia on April 28, 1841. The treacherous river had claimed an estimated 234 ships since its "discovery" in 1792 by Robert Gray, an American sea captain; Wilkes claimed that "mere description can give little idea of the terrors of the bar of the Columbia . . . the wildness of the scene, and the incessant roar of the waters, representing it as one of the most fearful sights that can possible meet the eye of the sailor." So fearful was it that Wilkes did not attempt to enter and instead took his two ships north to the straits of Juan de Fuca (the passage between Vancouver

Island and Washington's Olympic Peninsula), where they anchored at Port Discovery, near the eastern end of the straits. Wilkes described the Klallam Indians who met them there as a "filthy race" with "few of the comforts, and barely the necessaries of life," but they were sufficiently well provisioned to provide the expedition with venison, fowl, fish, and other seafood.

The ships then headed southeast into Puget Sound in search of the outpost maintained by the Hudson's Bay Company, a British fur-trading concern, at the mouth of the Nisqually River. En route they surveyed many bays and harbors, leading Wilkes to proudly observe that "there is no country in the world that possesses waters equal to these." Once again, Wilkes had reason to marvel at the generosity of the inhabitants: At Fort Nisqually, the hospitality of Alexander Anderson, the agent in charge, disarmed the Americans, who had been, according to Wilkes, "prepared to exert force" if the British questioned their right to be in the area. Instead, the captain found himself gratefully accepting Anderson's offer of horses and supplies for his several exploring parties, which fanned out, by boat and on horseback, to chart Puget Sound, the Cascade Mountains, and the Willamette Valley.

Wilkes himself led the Willamette Valley party, which also surveyed the Columbia as far east as Walla Walla. Although he admitted that his contingent of navy men,

While one member of a surveying party rests, another stretches in an attempt to measure a massive tree trunk in what Wilkes called the Oregon pine forest. In actuality, the majestic trees encountered there by the expedition and sketched here by Drayton were Sitka spruce or Douglas fir.

Drayton's depiction of Indians at Willamette Falls catching salmon during the fishes' annual run. "I never saw so many fish collected together before," Wilkes wrote in the narratives in appreciation of Native American fishing methods, "and the Indians are constantly employed in taking them."

after almost three years at sea, "were but sorry horsemen," Wilkes delighted in being once more on his home continent, on territory that he was certain would soon belong to the United States alone. He "felt that the land belonged to my country, that we were not strangers on the soil; and could not but take great interest in relation to its destiny," he recorded in his narratives. Abroad, Wilkes was frequently caustic about the landscape; in his own country (as he felt he was), he waxed euphoric, as in the following passage recording a view of the Columbia from Fort Vancouver, a British outpost: "The noble river can be traced in all its windings, for a long distance through the cultivated prairie, with its groves and clumps of trees; beyond the eye sweeps over an interminable forest, melting into a blue haze, from which Mount Hood, capped with its eternal snows, rises in great beauty." The surveying went well, and along the way Wilkes met and talked with numerous American settlers, whom he advised to refrain from any action against the British and patiently "wait until the government of the United States should throw its mantle over them."

The Wilkes party returned to Fort Nisqually near the end of June. There, Wilkes learned that the other survey work thus far had gone as well as his own, so when the

Fourth of July rolled around, he uncharacteristically re-
warded his men with "a full day's frolic." In uniforms
"white as snow, with happy and contented faces," the
seamen paraded past the fort with "flags flying and music
playing" and hailed their British hosts with three cheers,
the narratives recorded. Two brass howitzers fired salutes
from the grounds outside the fort, where an ox was bar-
becued and the sailors raced horses rented from the Indians
"like wild men to & fro over the plain," danced "like mad"
to the tune of a fiddle, and engaged in an impromptu
football game, presided over by a merry Wilkes, who
chimed in from the sidelines with shouts of "sail in, my
shipmates!" When he left the picnic site, the captain was
sent off, for one of the few times in the course of the
expedition, with three cheers from his men.

Less than two weeks later, on July 17, the *Peacock* and
the *Flying Fish* reached the mouth of the Columbia River.
They were more than 10 weeks overdue; for that reason,
perhaps, the next morning Hudson, in the larger ship,
tried to enter the river without the help of a local guide
and ran the *Peacock* onto the bar. Aboard the *Flying Fish*,
some distance to the leeward, Reynolds made the *Peacock*
"out to be hard and fast among the breakers, and as we
[came] nearer her we could see that she thumped and
lurched heavily, and that the Seas were striking her with
a fury that must soon break her to pieces. We gave her
up for lost from that moment." It "was soul sickening to
look on," he added; huge breakers were "rolling on to her
in awful force, and surging her on to the sandy bottom,
worse than ever she went on to the Ice." After trying
various stratagems, Hudson was at last forced to give the
order to abandon ship. With the aid of some Chinook
Indians, who were used to braving the rough waters in
their intricately carved canoes, all the *Peacock*'s men were
landed safely before it broke up, although one sailor suffered critical injuries when his boat capsized. All of the
expedition's entomological specimens, however, and

much of the work pertaining to Hawaii went down with the ship. "There is some consolation," one officer wrote, "in knowing that after the many narrow risks she has run this cruise . . . her fate ha[d] been prolonged until reaching her native shore."

Trapped offshore by the breakers, the *Flying Fish* was finally guided by Indian George, a local pilot, to Baker's Bay, the sheltered cove near where the *Peacock*'s survivors had been taken by the Chinook. Several Methodist missionaries who had witnessed the disaster from their settlement brought tents and provisions to the castaways, and the local Indians provided salmon and venison. After sending messengers to inform Wilkes of his situation, Hudson took 100 men from his wrecked ship 10 miles upriver, where they established an encampment of pine-branch huts and plank wigwams that they jovially dubbed "Peacockville." The *Flying Fish*, meanwhile, had been ordered to await Wilkes near Baker's Bay, where the *Vincennes* and the *Porpoise* arrived on August 6. Wilkes then sent his flagship on south to San Francisco Bay to survey it and the Sacramento River and took the two smaller ships, which were able to cross the bar, upriver to Peacockville.

From the deck of the Flying Fish, *which prudently remained outside the bar, Agate drew this picture of the wreck and abandonment of the* Peacock *at the mouth of the Columbia River on July 18, 1841.*

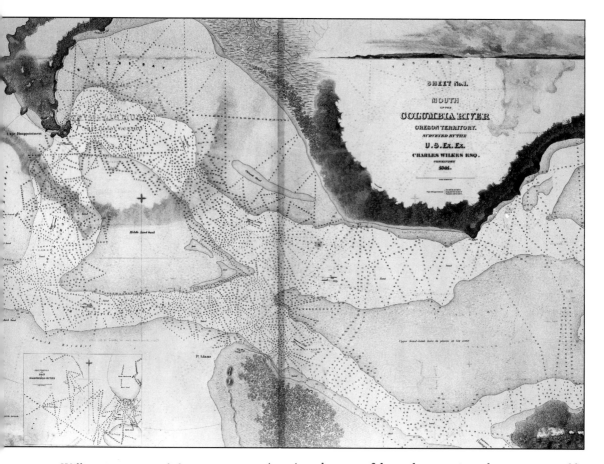

Wilkes came to regard the
surveying done in the Oregon
Country as the most important
performed by the expedition,
perhaps because it concerned the
United States's immediate
territorial ambitions. Seen here is
the survey chart for the mouth of
the Columbia River.

Any joy that was felt at the reunion there was quickly
dissipated. Wilkes was irked by the disaster and was worried
that he would not be able to complete the survey of the
Columbia, which he now termed the "most important
part" of the entire expedition, by the onset of the rainy
season. He was appalled that Hudson, even after the wreck,
had not moved the surveying work further along and "disgusted with the ignorance, idleness, want of thought, &
want of proper energy & exertion" shown by his men.
What little work Hudson had been able to carry out,
Wilkes wrote, had been done "without requisite knowledge
& comprehension of the duty to be performed." The captain vented his frustration in characteristic fashion: He

lambasted Hudson for the shipwreck and shabby surveying work, arrested two men, suspended three others, and denied two more permission to leave the squadron. "Verily I have many things to contend with," Wilkes confided to his journal. "Ignorance is not the least of them. . . . A Surveyor needs more patience than Job, with all his trials I require more resignation than he did." The expedition's commander had finally become "more . . . a monster than a man," Reynolds decided at about this time.

Driven by Wilkes's fury, the expedition succeeded in charting over 100 miles of the Columbia by October. Their most important work was a map entitled "Mouth of the Columbia River, Oregon Territory, 1841." Combined with John C. Frémont's map of the Rocky Mountains and regions westward from his survey of the following year, it provided the most comprehensive picture to date of the land from the Rockies to the Pacific. In the meantime, Wilkes had sent an overland party to San Francisco in early September. It reached John Sutter's spread on the American River on October 19, after about six weeks of travel; among the Oregon settlers who accompanied this party was a Mrs. Joel Walker, who thereby, it has been claimed, became the first white woman to reach California by an overland route.

Wilkes arrived in San Francisco Bay aboard the *Porpoise*, also on October 19. At the time, California was governed by Mexico—a state of affairs that Frémont, not long afterward, would do much to change—and as it did not impress Wilkes with "either its beauty or fertility," he did not plan to stay long. With the exception of the *Flying Fish*, which was finishing the Columbia River survey, the various ships and overland and surveying parties—the squadron now featured a new brig, the *Oregon*, purchased and renamed by Wilkes in the Northwest as a replacement for the *Peacock*—were reunited in San Francisco by October 28, and all concerned were making plans for the voyage home.

This street scene in the Southeast Asian city of Singapore, which was then part of a British East India Company territory of the same name, appeared in volume five of Wilkes's narratives. At Singapore, Wilkes decided to sell the plucky Flying Fish.

would proceed to the northwest in search of islands and atolls west and northwest of Hawaii and then to the Sea of Japan. A rendezvous was scheduled for Singapore no later than the first week of February 1842. Such a schedule meant that Wilkes's promise, made during the reenlistment crisis in Hawaii, to return the expedition to the east coast of the United States by the end of May 1842 could not be fulfilled. The enlisted men, Reynolds reported, resigned themselves "to be humbugged and delayed all the way home."

At Singapore in February, Wilkes decided to sell the *Flying Fish*. Badly battered from the travails of the expedition, it had almost sunk near Manila, and Wilkes feared it would not survive the passage around the Cape of Good Hope, Africa's southern tip. This decision, although prudent, was not popular. One officer felt the noble little vessel deserved "a place in our National Museum—if we ever have one." Instead, it was most likely used by its new owners to smuggle opium.

The remaining vessels of the South Seas Exploring Expedition departed Singapore on February 26. All concerned, according to Reynolds, assumed that they would rendezvous at Capetown, in South Africa, and then sail triumphantly home in tandem, but at Java, Wilkes revealed that the *Vincennes* alone would take the direct route to New York. The *Porpoise* and the *Oregon* were ordered to Rio de Janeiro, where, as Reynolds put it, they would "make some paltry magnetic experiments" and pick up five boxes of scientific specimens "light enough to be lifted by one hand." One officer estimated that this directive cost the government $10,000, but for Reynolds and most of his colleagues "the miserable reason" for what they regarded as a transparent ploy was "very plain." Wilkes, Reynolds reasoned, "did not wish to be detained by sailing in Company, and in separating to make sure that we should not arrive home before him," thereby ensuring for himself alone the expected hero's welcome.

But the captain's arrival in New York harbor on June 10, 1842, was greeted with a yawn of indifference. Almost four years had passed since the expedition set sail, and many more years than that had elapsed since it had been a topic of enthusiastic debate. Similar disinterest greeted the arrival, shortly afterward, of the *Porpoise* and the *Oregon*. To a large extent, the explorers had been forgotten by their countrymen. The New York *Tribune* attributed the public's lack of interest to ignorance, while another newspaper reported a widespread tendency to view the expedition as an "idle and useless" venture. Elected officials were equally apathetic, and the House of Representatives even refused to pass a resolution commending the expedition and its achievements. One of the few aspects of the voyage to capture the public's interest was the presence of Vendovi, the Fijian chief, aboard the *Vincennes*, but he had grown very ill during the course of the voyage and was taken from the flagship directly to a naval hospital, where he died after only a few hours. The New York

Agate's portrait of Vendovi, the Fijian chieftain whom Hudson convicted of murder and sentenced to exile in the United States. An expedition sailor described him as "about 35 years of age, tall and rather slender, [with] a countenance which belies his character—its expression is mild and benevolent." Wilkes believed that Vendovi's demise was hastened by his grief at the death by illness of Benjamin Vanderford, a member of the expedition who had befriended him.

Some scholars believe that the American novelist Herman Melville modeled the character Queequeg in Moby-Dick *on Ko-towa-towa, the Maori chief portrayed here by Agate. Scholars have also speculated that Melville's creation of the monomaniacal Captain Ahab was inspired by his interpretation of the character of Wilkes.*

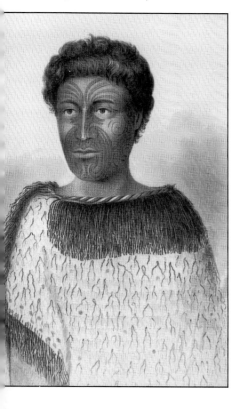

Herald speculated that his illness was a "consequence probably of having no human flesh to eat." (The scientifics had the Fijian's head pickled and added his skull to their ethnological collection.)

Part of the public's disillusionment was no doubt due to the sensational rumors that circulated concerning the tempestuous relationship between captain and crew. Three days after the arrival of the *Vincennes*, a reporter for the *Herald* wrote: "We understand that there is to be a nice mess dished up in a short time in the shape of court martials, courts of inquiry, [and] arranging of specimens. . . . It is said that there are at least a bushel and a half of charges already preferred against Lieut. Wilkes, the commander-in-chief." Less than a month after the full squadron's return, 23 court-martial charges were heard by a naval court convened aboard the USS *North Carolina*. One of the four junior officers thus tried was acquitted, two were found guilty of disrespect, and the fourth was dismissed from the service; but the trials were more significant for what they revealed about Wilkes's command. Some witnesses described Wilkes as "violent, overbearing, insulting, taxing forebearance to the last degree," and "offensive to a gentleman," although others testified to his unflagging devotion to duty and his "very prompt and energetic" manner.

The commander himself then faced a court-martial on charges—brought by the four that he had accused—that included oppression, cruelty, disobedience of orders, illegal punishments, violation of terms of enlistment, scandalous conduct tending to the destruction of good morals, and scandalous conduct unbecoming an officer. He attributed the charges to a personal vendetta on the part of incompetent officers who "had a determination of taking their revenge upon me" and did not expect to be treated fairly since his case was heard by a "picked court" that was "indisposed to do me justice." Nor, since "the press has teemed with that unqualified denunciation of me personally," did he expect vindication in the eyes of the public. Nevertheless, he was acquitted of all charges except illegal punishments, the accusations that he said caused him "the least anxiety." The court found that 17 of the 25 floggings he had ordered exceeded naval regulations and sentenced him to a public reprimand by the secretary of the navy.

The trials and the scandalous charges—most sensational among them the accusation that Wilkes had lied about the discovery of Antarctica—left a cloud over the expedition and its commander, but Wilkes pressed on, motivated by the belief that some of the expedition's most important work had not yet begun. For the next 35 years, Wilkes devoted the greatest part of his considerable energies to supervising the writing and compilation of the volumes explaining the voyage's scientific finds, writing his own scientific tomes, compiling his 5-volume *Narrative of the United States Exploring Expedition During the Years 1838, 1839, 1840, 1841, 1842,* and penning his autobiography. (During much of this time, he continued his career in the navy, finally receiving an official promotion to captain in 1855, and, in fulfillment of Mammy Reed's prognostication, an appointment as admiral in 1866. He was also court-martialed again, this time for intentionally leaking a self-promoting letter to the press during the course of a dispute with the secretary of the navy, an action that earned him a three-year suspension from the service.)

"I was equal to those who wanted to crush me and my work," Wilkes proudly proclaimed in the autobiography, which remained unfinished and unpublished at his death in February 1877, but his literary efforts brought him new battles and criticisms. His insistence on controlling every aspect of the publication of the official volumes of the expedition brought him into renewed conflict with the scientifics, and he fired several of them. Asa Gray, for example, took over for William Rich, who was undertrained for his task, in compiling the volumes on botany,

This photograph of the main building of the Smithsonian Institution—the so-called Castle on the Mall—was taken by Titian Peale in 1862. The Smithsonian was created to house the specimens collected by the South Seas Exploring Expedition, which the writer and philosopher Ralph Waldo Emerson called the "best sight in Washington" after the Capitol.

and Titian Peale's *Zoology* was withdrawn because of its inadequacy. Wilkes's own scientific efforts were uneven. His two-volume atlas of charts was generally excellent (and remained the standard resource for many of the Pacific regions until after World War II), his *Theory of Winds* much less so, and he was heavily and justly criticized for his habit, most evident in the narratives, of making un-credited use of the work of others. In the narratives, Wilkes incorporated material taken from secondary sources and the ships' logs and borrowed heavily, in the form of un-acknowledged verbatim quotations, from the private jour-nals he had insisted his men write and which he then impounded, yet he still credited himself as sole author. Many readers noticed and criticized the pastiche of styles thus represented within the text, and Wilkes's own writing, when evident, was remarked upon unfavorably for its woodenness, self-aggrandizement, and transparent at-tempts at self-justification. Congress, which had commis-sioned their publication, wound up ordering only 100 copies.

But Wilkes's literary work represented a triumph as well. The narratives constituted a rare look at naval life and the mysterious Pacific and as such inspired such great Ameri-can authors as James Fenimore Cooper and Herman Mel-ville, who purchased a complete set. (Queequeeg, the tattooed Pacific Island cannibal in Melville's whaling epic *Moby-Dick*, was modeled, in part, on a Maori chief Wilkes described.) The 19 volumes compiled by the sci-entifics and edited by him constituted exactly what he and many others had hoped the expedition would be: an an-nouncement to the nations of Europe that the United States was fast becoming their equal in scientific endeav-ors. Several broke significant new ground, most noticeably Dana's *Geology*, which in addition to demonstrating the truth of Darwin's hypothesis about the formation of vol-canic islands and coral atolls also anticipated the modern notions of plate tectonics and continental drift. John James

Audubon, the great American naturalist and wildlife painter, believed that the work of the scientifics "ought to come to the World of Science as least as brightly as the brightest rays of the Orb of Day [i.e. the sun] during the Mid-summer solstice." The more than 160,000 specimens that the scientifics returned with so overwhelmed the existing facilities for their storage and study that in 1856 a national museum—the Smithsonian Institution—was created in Washington, D.C., to house them. This, more than any frigate bird collected from a South Sea atoll or shoal charted off a Fiji isle, is the expedition's most important legacy, for it represented a belated and lasting recognition on the part of the federal government that the pursuit and acquisition of scientific knowledge is a legitimate and essential national interest.

The United States South Seas Exploring Expedition, the last expedition to circumnavigate the globe in sailing ships, thus constitutes a significant achievement, a triumph of courage, dedication, perseverance, and intellect. In leaky ships, serving under a commander whom they hated, in some of the most far-flung and dangerous regions of the globe, the men of the expedition accomplished prodigious feats of exploration. Three of their ships did not survive the voyage; 23 of their colleagues perished during it, a few during conflicts with native peoples, most from illness or accident. More than one-third—127 men—deserted. As regards the Antarctic expeditions in particular, Ian Cameron, a historian of exploration, be-

Its boats return to the San Jacinto *(at left), commanded by Wilkes, with the Confederate emissaries James Mason and John Slidell, who had just been removed from the British mail packet* Trent. *Wilkes's unilateral action in seizing the Confederate diplomats precipitated an international crisis.*

In 1848, Wilkes was awarded the Founder's Medal of the Royal Geographical Society of London, one of the most prestigious such organizations in the world, for the "zeal and intelligence with which he carried out the scientific exploring expedition intrusted to him," but his efforts went largely unappreciated in his own nation.

lieves that no "ships' companies, before or since, were ever asked to endure such terrible conditions."

As the expedition's commander, Wilkes deserves some share of the credit. Exactly how much continues to be debated; certainly for the rest of his days Wilkes's personality always overshadowed his accomplishments, and when he died many obituaries failed to mention the expedition at all, dwelling instead on a later controversial incident in his career, the notorious Trent Affair. (During the U.S. Civil War, Wilkes, acting without orders, took it upon himself to stop a British ship, the *Trent*, and take from it two Confederate envoys bound for a diplomatic conclave in England. His precipitous action created an international incident and almost succeeded in bringing Britain into the war on the side of the Confederacy.) It is difficult to find in this oversight a bitter historical irony; those whose backs were stung and stripped raw by the bite of a cat-o'-nine-tails or whose work was claimed as his own might be inclined to believe that in obscurity, rather than infamy, Wilkes got better than he deserved. Yet, however one feels about his methods, he succeeded, against considerable odds, in carrying out his mission, and one may wonder if, even despite his obvious shortcomings, Wilkes may have been the only naval officer suitable for the job. Certainly, no other navy man of the day demonstrated a similar commitment to science. One must consider the assessment of him given by Dana in 1847, nine years after the geologist complained of the "naval servitude" imposed on the scientifics by the hard-driving commander. "Wilkes[,] although overbearing and conceited," Dana wrote, "exhibited through the whole cruise a wonderful degree of energy and was bold even to rashness in exploration. . . . I much doubt if, with any other commander that could have been selected, we should have fared better or lived together more harmoniously, and I am confident that the Navy does not contain a more daring or driving officer."

Further Reading

Bixby, William. *The Forgotten Voyage of Charles Wilkes*. New York: McKay, 1966.

Cameron, Ian. *Lost Paradise: The Exploration of the Pacific*. Topsfield, MA: Salem House, 1987.

Cleaver, Anne Hoffmann, and E. Jeffrey Stann. *Voyage to the Southern Ocean: The Letters of Lieutenant William Reynolds from the U.S. Exploring Expedition, 1838–1842*. Annapolis: U.S. Naval Institute, 1988.

Dodge, Ernest S. *Beyond the Capes: Pacific Exploration from Captain Cook to the "Challenger" (1776–1877)*. Boston: Little, Brown, 1971.

Friis, Herman R. *The Pacific Basin: A History of Its Geographical Exploration*. New York: American Geographical Society, 1967.

Goetzmann, William H. *New Lands, New Men: America and the Second Great Age of Discovery*. New York: Viking Press, 1986.

Hafertepe, Kenneth. *America's Castle: The Evolution of the Smithsonian Building and Its Institution, 1840–1878*. Washington, DC: Smithsonian Institution Press, 1984.

Harris, Edward D. *John Charles Frémont and the Great Western Reconnaissance*. New York: Chelsea House, 1990.

Jenkins, John. *Explorations and Adventures in and Around the Pacific and Antarctic Oceans*. New York: Hurst, N. d.

Johnson, Robert E. *Thence Round Cape Horn*. Annapolis: U.S. Naval Institute, 1963.

Poesch, Jessie. *Titian Ramsay Peale 1799–1885 and His Journals of the Wilkes Expedition*. Philadelphia: American Philosophical Society, 1961.

Shelton, R. A. *Captain James Cook After Two Hundred Years*. London: The British Museum, 1969.

Silverberg, Robert. *Stormy Voyager: The Story of Charles Wilkes*. New York: Lippincott, 1968.

Stanton, William. *The Great United States Exploring Expedition of 1838–1842*. Berkeley: University of California Press, 1975.

Tyler, David B. *The Wilkes Expedition: The First United States Exploring Expedition (1838–1842)*. Philadelphia: American Philosophical Society, 1968.

Viola, Herman J., and Carolyn Margolis, eds. *Magnificent Voyagers: The U.S. Exploring Expedition, 1838–1842*. Washington, DC: Smithsonian Institution Press, 1985.

Warren, Gordon H. *Fountain of Discontent: The Trent Affair and the Freedom of the Seas*. Boston: Northeastern University Press, 1981.

Wilkes, Charles. *Autobiography of Rear Admiral Charles Wilkes, U.S. Navy 1798–1877*. Edited by William James Morgan, et al. Washington, DC: Naval History Division, Department of the Navy, 1978.

———. *The Narrative of the United States Exploring Expedition During the Years 1838, 1839, 1840, 1841, 1842*. Vols. 1–5. Philadelphia: Lea and Blanchard, 1845.

Chronology

1768–79	Captain James Cook circumnavigates the world, exploring extensively in the South Pacific
April 3, 1798	Charles Wilkes born in New York City
1825	U.S. president John Quincy Adams recommends the creation of a U.S. exploring expedition
1836	Congress authorizes the United States South Seas Exploring Expedition
1838	Lieutenant Charles Wilkes offered command of the expedition due to the poor health of Commodore Thomas ap Catesby Jones; the flagship *Vincennes* and five other ships set sail from Hampton Roads, Virginia
Jan.–April 1839	The expedition leaves Rio de Janeiro and rounds Cape Horn; brutal cold stops Wilkes's first polar voyage short of Antarctica
May 1839–Feb. 1840	*Sea Gull* lost between Valparaiso and Orange Harbor; Wilkes promotes himself to the rank of captain; the expedition surveys and maps the Tuamotu group, Samoa, and Tahiti; departs from Sydney, Australia, on second Antarctic voyage, during which Wilkes demonstrates the existence of Antarctica as a continent
March–Aug. 1840	The expedition explores and charts Fiji; Wilkes leads full-scale assault on the island of Malolo in retaliation for the killing of two sailors
Sep. 1840–April 1841	The fleet reaches Hawaii, where it winters; Wilkes leads expedition to the summit of Mauna Loa

May–Oct. 1841	The expedition explores and charts Puget Sound, the Cascade Mountains, the Willamette Valley, and much of the Columbia River; *Peacock* wrecked at the mouth of the Columbia
Nov. 1841–May 1842	Return voyage; *Flying Fish* sold in Singapore
June 1842	Aboard the *Vincennes*, Wilkes arrives in New York harbor to public indifference
July–Aug. 1842	Court-martial proceedings aboard the USS *North Carolina* cast into doubt Wilkes's competence and honesty
1842–56	Specimens collected by the expedition's "scientifics" exhibited to great public acclaim, leading to the creation of the Smithsonian Institution
1842–77	Wilkes writes or edits his own five-volume narrative of the expedition, his unpublished autobiography, nine volumes of scientific work pertaining to the expedition, and nine volumes of maps
1848	Awarded Founder's Medal of the Royal Geographic Society of London for his work with U.S. Exploring Expedition
Nov. 1861	International contretemps occurs when Wilkes, now a commander in the Union navy, seizes Confederate envoys from a British ship
Feb. 1877	Wilkes dies

Index

Picture Credits

Cheri Wolfe has a B.A. from Princeton University and an M.A. in American studies from the University of Texas at Austin, where she is an assistant instructor in American studies and is working on her doctorate in the field.

William H. Goetzmann holds the Jack S. Blanton, Sr., Chair in History at the University of Texas at Austin, where he has taught for many years. The author of numerous works on American history and exploration, he won the 1967 Pulitzer and Parkman prizes for his *Exploration and Empire: The Role of the Explorer and Scientist in the Winning of the American West, 1800–1900*. With his son William N. Goetzmann, he coauthored *The West of the Imagination*, which received the Carr P. Collins Award in 1986 from the Texas Institute of Letters. His documentary television series of the same name received a blue ribbon in the history category at the American Film and Video Festival held in New York City in 1987. A recent work, *New Lands, New Men: America and the Second Great Age of Discovery*, was published in 1986 to much critical acclaim.

Michael Collins served as command module pilot on the *Apollo 11* space mission, which landed his colleagues Neil Armstrong and Buzz Aldrin on the moon. A graduate of the United States Military Academy, Collins was named an astronaut in 1963. In 1966 he piloted the *Gemini 10* mission, during which he became the third American to walk in space. The author of several books on space exploration, Collins was director of the Smithsonian Institution's National Air and Space Museum from 1971 to 1978 and is a recipient of the Presidential Medal of Freedom.